NOT ON MY WATCH!

The Fight to End Human Trafficking

"Ordinary People, Unthinkable Stories, and the Forgotten Cries for Freedom"

MALCOLM ALLEN

Not on My Watch!

Copyright © 2019 by **Malcolm Allen**

Web: **www.Unconditional.org**
ISBN: 9781072259541

CONTENTS

HUMAN TRAFFICKING: TWENTY-FIRST-CENTURY SLAVERY

"None of us, is truly free, while others remain enslaved."

- Archbishop Desmond Tutu

One of the most important documents in America's history is Abraham Lincoln's Emancipation Proclamation. It freed the captive workers of the Confederacy and held the promise of greater rights for all. It was a huge step forward, but American slavery didn't end with the Civil War. Despite the South's surrender on the battlefield, slavery endured in other, less visible forms throughout the United States. Americans of African ancestry were still regulated by a system of Jim Crow laws that segregated and controlled them. Traditions and legal limitations still enslaved many women and children. Laborers from China were brought here against their will, becoming corporate slaves to the companies building the transcontinental railroads.

Finally, a century after Lincoln's Proclamation, the Civil Rights Movement made great strides toward curbing this post–Civil War enslavement. Yet in some pockets of the world, and even in twenty-first-century America, slavery has persisted. The methods of enslavement have changed, but the wrongs continue. The most common name we have for today's business of enslaving, transporting, and selling people is "human trafficking."

Modern slavery has a multitude of causes and takes a variety of forms. In Uganda, nine-year-old Concy found himself forced into service as a young soldier in a rebel army that was committed to the overthrow of that country's government. "My mother and I were asleep in our hut when they barged in and woke us up by kicking down the door," Concy writes in an essay on equality-now.org. "Five men caught us right away. One man held me down, ripped off my blouse, and tied me up. I watched in horror as another man beat my mother badly." These captors soon separated Concy from his family and marched him off to war. There he joined thousands of other boy soldiers.

These rebels understood the vulnerabilities of the young. They knew they could force children to do almost anything. Most children don't have enough experience or education to understand their plight. Their minds can be formed and changed by simple indoctrination. The rebels established their authority through violence, then reinforced it with threats and commands. Any rebellious child quickly learned that when these soldiers made threats, they weren't bluffing. If any boy were to disobey a command, punishment would be swift, painful, and sometimes fatal. When Concy had suffered enough, and seen others die at the hands of their commanders, he fell into line. He was forced to kill, and sometimes he was ordered to rape girls who were as young, or even younger, than he was. Back in camp Concy was continually raped by his own squadron commander.

In Southeast Asia, Natalie was trapped into a life of prostitution. Forced into service in an illegal brothel, she escaped after just a few months. To avoid recapture, Natalie fled to Australia, but history repeated itself. She was caught in an unending cycle of despair.

She'd borrowed money for her escape from Asia, but when she reached what she hoped would be freedom in Australia, her creditors forced her to work off what she owed them in a "legal" brothel. Once her captors had her working, they had ways to ensure that her debt could never be fully paid. They took almost every cent she earned, charging her for items such as bed sheets, and services that included electricity and even bathroom visits. "If you were five minutes late, they charged you $50," she says. Instead of seeing her debt shrink, she watched as it mounted up every day, draining all hope from her future. Once she realized that they didn't intend to free her until she was useless, she began to plan her escape. It took her seven years, but she finally broke free of them.

When twelve-year-old Barbara got swept up by human traffickers, she had already suffered abuse at the hands of a family member. After running away from her home in Northern Virginia, she was soon walking D.C.'s streets, unsure of what to do next. That's where the traffickers found her. Once they'd ensnared her, they moved her to New York, where they forced her to become a prostitute. "During my time on the streets of New York I was abused, shot, stabbed, raped, kidnapped, trafficked, beaten, addicted to drugs, jailed, and more all before I was eighteen years old," she recently told an interviewer. Finally, Barbara managed to flee and start the long road to healing. For victims like Barbara, this cure is a process that never ends. You get better, but every day has an edge.

Barbara returned to her home state of Virginia, then got married and adopted a little girl. For years she kept her story secret, but now she feels a parental obligation to share her story with her daughter. She's done that, and she's also posted her account of her years in bondage online. Barbara is determined to keep history from repeating itself in her daughter's life. She hopes her posted story will serve as a warning to the girls in the next generation.

The experiences of these and many other victims show us how the human trafficking crisis stretches around the world. No one is immune to its destruction. These traffickers flout the law. The effects of their crimes spill across national borders. They spread violence and disease, leaving millions of victims in their wake. The United Nations' International Labour Organization (ILO) estimates that twenty-one million people live in a condition of slavery each year, providing human traffickers with $150 billion in annual income. The enslaved victims get nothing.

Slavery steals hope from the human heart, robbing its prey of their dreams. It sucks the life from its victims, leaving many broken beyond repair. It chops up families, decimates villages, and infects whole societies. When a nation accepts the existence of slavery within its borders, it invites destruction.

Most human trafficking is organized, as tasks are broken down and delegated to those with the necessary skills. Some traffickers specialize in recruitment and capture, while others train and discipline their helpless victims. In some cases, guards and overseers are brought in to manage these captives. Other times enslaved workers are held in place by fear for themselves, or for their families. These trapped people work in brothels, factories, and even private homes. Some labor on farms and plantations, just as many enslaved African-Americans did before they found a path to freedom.

As most of us have learned here in America, the road to freedom can often be long and bumpy. Though Lincoln freed the enslaved African-Americans of the Confederacy, his proclamation was just the beginning of a process that goes on to this day. Before he died, Lincoln managed to give legal freedom to all captive Americans with the passage of a constitutional amendment outlawing slavery throughout the land.

This was followed by legal guarantees for basic rights, like voting and due process of law.

Legislators put these great ideas into the law books, but for many years most white Americans ignored statutes guaranteeing freedom for these once-enslaved citizens. White folks in the defeated Confederacy replaced the old institution of slavery with their Black Codes and Jim Crow laws. The earlier system had allowed individual white folks to "own" individual black folks. Jim Crow forced the entire African-American population into "servitude" to the white race. It was based on the idea that one race could own another. To put it bluntly, under Jim Crow, American slavery switched from retail to wholesale, stripping a vital part of identity from each African-American. It would be another century before these chains were finally broken.

The online encyclopedia, Wikipedia.com, describes three main forms of modern slavery. The first is "Bonded Labor," which is the least known, yet most prevalent form of twenty-first-century enslavement. It includes those working off endless debts, and poor workers who are forced to agree to long-term, low-pay contracts. Many prostitutes and farmworkers fall into this category.

"Forced labor" happens when captives are coerced into working regular jobs for nothing but substandard food, clothing, and shelter. A lot of these laborers toil on farms and in factories, while others serve as janitors, drivers, cooks, or even miners. The ILO says that these coerced workers earn their masters over $31 billion per year in profits. Meanwhile most of the workers never see a dime.

"Child Labor" can take many forms, and because it is not always abusive or unjust, it creates gray areas. A little girl who learns to help in her parents' corner grocery store might enjoy what she's doing as she also gains valuable insights about the workplace. The same might be true of her older brother who delivers grocery orders on his bicycle. Though their parents must be careful not to overwork these kids, this kind of experience is often healthy and educational. Children can get a humane and effective introduction to business, while taking on greater responsibilities and earning their own money.

But child labor is also a favorite activity of human traffickers. The labor they profit from is a very different kind of work, and these traffickers aren't interested in teaching kids anything. They prefer that their victims be ignorant and unquestioning. They use fear to assert their power. Most children become docile in the face of authority. Boys are usually the first to go into the fields and factories. Some work construction, and others are placed in the sex trade. Young girls are sold into service as prostitutes, maids, kitchen helpers, and some follow the boys into factories and onto farms. They live with the daily horrors of sexual assault, physical abuse, and psychological manipulation.

In the chapters that follow we will hear these victims speak. They will tell us grim stories that recount the sorry details of their experiences as enslaved workers. Their stories are real, and well-documented. Their experiences are not unique. Each enslaved worker's story is representative of millions of others. Together their descriptions of their individual circumstances will reveal the bigger picture. Human trafficking is a worldwide scourge. It affects everyone, including you, your friends, and your coworkers. The plastic doll you buy your daughter might have been crafted by a little Chinese girl working fourteen-hour days in a Manchurian sweatshop. The vegetables in your freezer could have been harvested by enslaved field hands in South America or Asia. Your reclusive neighbor might not allow his new wife to learn English because he doesn't want her to find out about her legal rights here in the U.S.

Most of us see ourselves as just, and we like to think of our country as one that is dedicated to freedom. Yet few of us consider all the American dollars that end up in the pockets of these human traffickers. We don't like to be reminded that we play a role in this. Most of us ignore the crisis or hope it will go away. We close our eyes, then blindly reach for products manufactured by captive workers. We hear of girls who are sold into forced marriages, boys who are lured into armies, and poor people who are coerced into working off impossibly huge debts. We shake our heads and agree that something should be done. Then, a moment later, we forget our vague resolve, and buy a cup of coffee whose beans were harvested by an eight-year-old plantation worker in South America. It often seems that we prefer to stay ignorant, but evading the problem only guarantees that it will get worse.

We must pay more attention, and act to end this stain on the human spirit. In our own country we should demand the passage of laws against the outrage of human trafficking. We should ban the sale of domestic products made by coerced labor and halt the import of slave-produced goods from other countries. We might volunteer in organizations that oppose this modern bondage by promoting effective action. We can also educate our children, telling them what to watch for, and how to protect themselves from predators who would take them as captives. We should also teach kids to respect each other, and to understand the responsibilities every citizen has in a free society.

We live in a country that strives to be a beacon of freedom for all people in all nations of the world. We think of ourselves as citizens in the freest country on the planet. We treasure our rights, protecting them from slow erosion and sudden attack. But if we want to light the way for others, we must begin with ourselves. What follows in these pages can help readers make that beginning.

Though modern slavery infects the whole world, it can be curbed, and finally ended. Slavery was once openly practiced everywhere, with few people protesting or questioning its effects. Leaders encouraged it, philosophers justified it, and slaveholders defended it to the death. Those days are gone. Today no nations officially sanction slavery. Instead they deny its existence. Modern slavery fades into the background, which often allows it to hide in plain sight. Sometimes all it takes to stop it is exposure. Once everyone can see it, the perpetrators are embarrassed, shamed, and often even jailed.

Here you will see the true faces of human trafficking. Learn to recognize what it is, and how it works. If we all join, we can end the scourge, and spread freedom to all the world's citizens. We can start by listening to those who have experienced slavery. Once we recognize it for what it really is, we can answer the cries from all the world's enslaved people. Like all humans everywhere, they yearn to be free.

SLAVES TO THE WORLD

"Our lives begin to end the day we become silent about things that matter."

-Dr. Martin Luther King

Holly Austin Smith was a fourteen-year-old girl in New Jersey who'd just graduated from middle school. Looking to her future, she was terrified of high school. She worried about losing friends who would be going to other schools, and she'd heard stories about girls who were assaulted in high school hallways. She was concerned about her marks and wondered if she was smart enough. Most of all she worried about boys. Would they like her? Hate her? Would she find one who would fall in love with her? Would she fall in love with him? Like a million other fourteen-year-olds, Holly wanted to grow up, get noticed, and find the happy life she'd dreamed about.

That's when she met the man at the mall. His name was Greg. He was older, wiser, and everything he said was exactly what she wanted to hear. According to Greg, Holly didn't need high school. She was far wiser than her years. She looked like a twenty-year-old model. She could be on television and appear in magazines. With her looks every photographer would want to take her picture. Every designer would want her to model the latest fashions. Wouldn't it be great to be a star?

Holly took the bait, arranging to meet Greg again, and go with him to pursue her dreams. He promised to buy her new outfits and take her to a dance club in Atlantic City. Once they were on their way, he began getting pushy. He had dye for her hair and wanted her to wear sexy outfits and high heels. He introduced her to an older girl who coached her, but Holly still couldn't see where this was leading.

It led to the streets of Atlantic City where Holly was forced into prostitution. After suffering the traumas of being a sex slave, she finally caught the eye of a cop. She was picked up wearing the revealing outfit of a prostitute. Getting the opportunity to talk to the police should have been Holly's salvation, but she quickly learned that the legal system was set up to be just another chapter in her horror story.

"Unfortunately, I wasn't immediately seen as a victim of a crime," she writes on her web site. "I was a criminal, a juvenile delinquent, and I was arrested… The most painful part of this experience wasn't what happened to me in Atlantic City, it was the way I was treated after Atlantic City—by law enforcement and even hospital staff."

They weren't concerned about her abductors, whom they saw simply as small-time pimps. The police, doctors, and other professionals decided that Holly was one more girl whose bad behavior had gone over the legal line into criminality. Their treatment of her, added to the trauma she'd survived, pushed her to the brink of suicide. The man who'd lured her into captivity was caught, but he served only a year in prison. Nevertheless, Holly survived her grim odyssey, and emerged from it to become one of our nation's strongest voices against human trafficking. "I'm passionate about sharing my story and working with front-line professionals," she tells readers. "By understanding my mindset and needs as a young victim of sex trafficking, professionals will be better equipped to recognize and respond to this victim population."

Holly understands what we all must learn, that this can happen anywhere, including right here in America. Her story is an American example of what's exploded into a global plague. It finds victims of all ages and nationalities.

Dee Dee was four years old when her father started selling her to men. These men were pedophiles who paid Dee Dee's father so that they could molest his daughter. All of this happened in a developing country our news media couldn't name due to potential threats to Dee Dee's safety. Her father would watch as the men got in bed with her. He claimed he was staying in the room for her benefit; he didn't want these men to hurt her. His real concern was probably the lost income any injury might cause, but Dee Dee didn't realize this until years later. "It was confusing," she said in a recent interview. "He was protecting me, but he was exploiting me."

The men would leave, and Dee Dee's father would tuck her in, much like a normal parent might. In an ugly twist on the role of a good father, he was always encouraging, commenting favorably on her work. He told her she should be proud of herself, and to keep it up. As she grew older, other men wanted her. Sometimes they added gifts to the fee. Dee Dee's father encouraged this. Though her mother learned something about one lone incident, her discovery didn't help Dee Dee. Ignorant of her husband's participation in the transaction, the poor woman reported the "customer" to the police. Before the police could arrest this man, Dee Dee's father tipped him off, and the man slipped out of the country. After that her father was more careful. He continued to profit from his exploitation of Dee Dee until she turned eighteen and left home.

Dee Dee didn't fully understand what had happened to her until long after she'd finally left home. Despite developing eating disorders, and her descent into an abusive relationship, Dee Dee had to go into therapy before she could see her life clearly. Only then could she recognize the difference between the world she had known, and a healthy life, free of abuse and deception. "It never even dawned on me that I was a victim," Dee Dee said. "It was what I had always known."

Julio and Jose were underage undocumented immigrants in Salt Lake City. These two friends and fellow high school students roomed together in a dorm-like hostel, where both soon met a man named Victor R. Victor claimed to be the protector of Latino boys in their Salt Lake neighborhood. Now, years later, both young men describe relationships that had nothing to do with protection. Instead they tell interviewers how Victor sexually abused them, while recruiting them to be his drug "mules" (people who transport drugs into places where the drug dealers can't or won't go). Investigators would eventually charge Victor with sending these enslaved boys into high schools and middle schools to peddle drugs to kids even younger than they were.

"He would say he could help, offer protection," says Jose. "If you wanted to go to the park or elsewhere nothing would happen to you. He says he was the protector of this area of Salt Lake."

Threats and isolation were basic parts of Victor's operation. "I was the only one who knew what he was doing," says Jose. "I could never go to police... If I did, he said he would kill these boys."

The police didn't know why Victor decided to target Salt Lake City, but when they investigated his background, they learned that he'd been involved in human trafficking long before he got to Utah. He too was an illegal, and in California the authorities had deported him to his native Mexico several times. He just kept coming back into the States. He traveled any way he could, including by boat, truck, or plane. Every time he arrived in the U.S., he brought more victims. He was a "coyote," which is something like a "mule." It's what human traffickers call those people who do the actual transporting across national borders. Victor brought in illegals by the dozen. He brought some in by the truckload, and herded others on foot. Often, he got paid twice—by the immigrant boys who thought they were buying freedom, and the men who were buying the boys from him.

Now that Victor has been found guilty of various trafficking-related felonies, he will serve many years in American prison before they send him back home. "Now that I know he's in jail I feel great that he's in there," Julio says. "I'm happy for other kids who [had it] worse than me."

Unfortunately, these stories are not unique. Pedophilia and drugs are at the root of many human trafficking cases. Other victims are forced into working in factories and fields.

Daniel came to the States on an H-2A visa, but when he realized he was stuck working for virtually nothing in terrible conditions, he appealed to his employers. They reminded him that his visa was in their hands. If they fired him, or if he quit, he would lose his status as a legal foreign worker. Finally, Daniel got many of his fellow workers interested in acting. They were all in the same bind. Acting together, they appealed to a charitable organization that helped them get a lawyer. After the lawyer intervened, the workers could leave the farm safely, and officials began a full investigation of the whole operation.

Sergio also came here legally, hoping to use his legal status as the first step to U.S. citizenship. He wanted to establish himself financially, then bring the rest of his family here. He found a man who was willing to help him reach that dream. The man promised Sergio a good job on a farm. He would get free housing, meals, good money, reasonable hours, and extra pay for overtime.

None of these promises panned out. Instead Sergio worked long hours, never got a day off, received no work breaks, and earned far less pay than he'd agreed to. Without any other resources, Sergio couldn't leave. The food was barely edible, and the living area that he shared with many others was filthy. He had no access to a bathroom or clean running water. He felt his captors should solve these problems, or he would have no choice but to try to escape. He suspected that his captors would go to almost any lengths to stop him. If they allowed him to go, they knew that others would follow. Once these victims were free it seemed inevitable that one would tell the authorities.

Sergio started by speaking to his supervisor. This man told Sergio he was lucky to be there, and that if he continued complaining, he would be barred from future employment anywhere in the U.S. His employers were holding Sergio's immigration documents, and now they refused to give those back to him. That's when he called an immigration hotline for advice. The people at the hotline listened to his story, and helped Sergio get a lawyer.

With the lawyer's help, Sergio escaped from the fields. Though it took some time, he was even able to recover some of the wages they'd promised him. He is now on course to become an American citizen. Eventually he would like to help others who find themselves in the same situation. He knows there are plenty out there.

Sergio and Daniel could stand up to their captors because they were in the U.S. legally, but those who come without the necessary documents have far fewer options.

Raul arrived here with no money or papers of any kind. As an illegal immigrant he had limited options, and when he got the chance to pick vegetables in North Carolina, he jumped at it. There he lived with six other men in a room in a labor camp. They and many others all shared bathroom and shower facilities. The rooms were cramped, and every bed was always filled.

The place was dirty, freezing, and allowed no privacy. Every day these men worked in the fields, using toxic pesticides, and operating dangerous machinery.

Without legal papers Raul wasn't allowed to quit, not even to go back home to Mexico. "I have not seen my children in over five years," he told a reporter. "I make these sacrifices, so they don't have to." This is the dream of every immigrant parent, but Raul is caught in a nightmare. At last report, he was still a captive in the illegal net of agricultural slavery.

Slaves like Dee Dee, Julio, Daniel, Sergio, and Raul are typical. Their exploiters make huge profits off their labor because enslaved workers require little pay and never get any benefits. Globally, the average cost of a slave is $90. About 80% of these captive people are used for sex, but many of them are forced to provide other services. Most victims work in factories or fields, and some are then expected to provide sexual services in their "off hours." The UN estimates that there are at least twenty million enslaved workers worldwide at any given time. Some remain slaves throughout their lives, while some of the luckier ones escape within weeks, or even days. Between six hundred thousand and eight hundred thousand of these captive people are here in the United States. 80% are female, and half are children.

Slave labor often starts early. Even here in the U.S. those who are underage usually enter the sex trade before their thirteenth birthday. Enslaved laborers on farms and in factories start even younger, often by the age of eight. The International Labour Organization estimates that around the world 11.4 million women and girls live in slavery, compared to 9.5 million males. Almost half of these live in, or are illegally carried into, the world's more affluent nations.

Obviously, the United States is not immune. Despite our country's stated commitment to freedom, fairness, and justice, we are home to about 4% of the world's enslaved people. This closely corresponds to our overall percentage of the world's population, so, unfortunately, we are doing our share.

The job of catching the slave traders isn't easy. Even when a human trafficking operation is exposed, its perpetrators may live in some other country, beyond the reach of the law. The criminals who transport and/or supervise these captives often set up escape routes in case of raids. When law enforcement must choose between chasing fleeing suspects, and securing the lives and health of the victims, most officers follow guidelines set by federal agencies. Those guidelines put the needs of the victims first.

An FBI website shows law enforcement's perspective on this crisis. It states: "The majority of human trafficking victims in our cases are U.S. citizens, and we take a victim-centered approach in investigating such cases, which means that ensuring the needs of the victims take precedence over all other considerations." In other words, they help the victims first, and only chase the traffickers when it's clear that the victims are safe and free. This is the best and most humane approach, but it often allows the traffickers to escape and resume their work.

Here in the U.S. we tend to think of human trafficking as an activity of organized crime, and our assumption is often true. The job of smuggling a constant stream of human labor across guarded borders requires recruiters, drivers, vehicles, payoffs, and buyers. Someone must make the deals and manage the finances. That's an ongoing criminal enterprise, which is the definition of "organized crime." When "coyotes" truck in dozens of illegal immigrants, and force them to work in the fields, or a pimp ensnares young women into drug addiction and isolation, these are also organized efforts targeting many buyers and victims. But some of our human traffickings is much more personal. Some selfish people engage in human exploitation because it's cheap, and others find it to be a handy way to buy a victim who can satisfy their sadistic urges.

That was the case when Sandra Bearden, a housewife from Laredo, Texas, traveled south of the border to find the perfect servant girl. There she began the process of enslaving a Mexican preteen named Maria. Sandra had come from Mexico herself many years earlier. Here in the States she'd prospered, marrying a native-born Texan, having a child, and settling into a nice suburban home in Laredo. The house was big, freshly painted, and surrounded by a perfectly manicured lawn. Sandra didn't like housework, and she also felt she needed a nanny for the Beardens' four-year-old son. Wanting a docile, obedient employee she traveled back to the land of her birth. She knew that was her best bet for finding a compliant girl who wouldn't cost much—one in desperate circumstances. She settled on twelve-year-old Maria, a child living in dire poverty with her parents in Veracruz.

Sandra painted a rosy picture, appealing to Maria's parents' dreams. They wanted their daughter to have a future. Sandra could take Maria north, teach her skills, and provide her with a good education. In return Maria would do some housework and act as the Bearden boy's nanny. In addition, Sandra would pay Maria's parents a lump sum which was more money than they had ever seen in their lives. Once the parents were taken care of, Sandra smuggled the child across the border. From then on, she held Maria captive in the Bearden family's home in Texas.

It was only two months later that police got a call about something going on at the Bearden residence. Neighbors had seen strange and horrible things going on in the backyard. The caller reported seeing a young girl shackled to a pole. From a distance this captive girl looked to be injured and may be malnourished. The caller described what was visible in graphic terms. Investigators arrived on the scene within minutes and found Maria. She was emaciated, dehydrated, and covered with cuts and bruises. Her eyes were infected from the effects of pepper spray, one of Sandra's favorite forms of "discipline." As if that weren't bad enough, there was evidence of even greater injuries. The housewife and mother had also hit Maria with brooms and bottles, and then sexually assaulted her with a gardening tool.

Sandra tried blaming it on cultural differences. She then claimed she had simply been correcting the girl for trying to abuse their young son. She didn't have a shred of evidence. When doctors examined Maria, they said she probably wouldn't have lived another week in the condition they'd found her in. She certainly wasn't capable of abusing anyone, not even a small child. Sandra was tried, convicted, and sentenced to life in prison.

"This is an ugly and often invisible problem," says star- activist, Jada Pinkett Smith, who produced the documentary, Rape for Profit. The film chronicles some of the worst abuses in sex trafficking. Smith is just one of the many celebrities who've been touched by this global crisis.

The price of human trafficking is paid with human lives. For every enslaved worker who escapes and thrives, many more barely survive and are scarred for life. Far too many enslaved people die at the hands of their captors. When packed into the backs of trucks some victims die of heat prostration. Others succumb to beatings, malnutrition, or exposure. All are subjected to the callous cruelty of those who treat them as if they were subhuman. This is as true in Texas as it is in Thailand.

BABIES FOR SALE AND CHILDREN AT WORK

"I have found that, to make a contented slave, it is necessary to make a thoughtless one. It is necessary to darken his moral and mental vision, and, as far as possible, to annihilate the power of reason."

-Frederick Douglass

In India almost two decades ago a thirteen-year-old girl, Phulmani, found herself sold into slavery. A man had lured her from her home village and brought her to India's capital, the city of Delhi. For a year she worked there as a domestic servant, but she was quickly growing up. When her captors saw this, they came up with a more profitable use for her. Though at first, it seemed as if they wanted her to become a prostitute, she soon realized that was only a part of their plan.

With no form of birth control and constant sex, Phulmani soon got pregnant. After having her first baby, she learned her captors' ultimate goal. They sold her baby on the black market, and put Phulmani back to work, peddling her services to their clients for their own profit and the johns' pleasure. Soon she was pregnant again, which suited her captors just fine. "They treated me like a money minting machine," she told interviewers. "My will never mattered to them. All they wanted was me to deliver babies for [sale]." She did this six times, and never knew anything about where her babies were taken. She only knew they were gone. To this day she has no way to contact her lost children.

Phulmani didn't escape until she was thirty. That's when a human rights group rescued her. As she finally came to understand the full extent of the torture she'd suffered, she filed an official complaint with India's Child Welfare Committee. It was the first time they had ever heard of a child prostitute being used for forced surrogacy (breeding babies for sale on the black market), but it would not be the last.

Since then India's authorities have discovered that many girls from other districts have been captured for the same purpose. One elderly man, Jagatram Mahato, who comes from a village named Arahasa, told interviewers that some of the girls from his village had been enslaved. Their new "masters" had turned these young girls into breeders, much like Phulmani. As the babies were born, they were taken from the girls, and sold like any other contraband on the black market. "Some of [these girls] even gave birth to their children in the village," Mahato said. "Later the agents came and took the babies."

This practice combines several basic forms of human trafficking. Many of these girls are captured, or lured into slavery, before they are old enough to conceive. At that point they are child slaves. Like Phulmani, they begin as domestic servants in well-to-do homes. These children clean, cook, and perform other chores, making them into classic examples of domestic enslavement. When they begin to mature, their captors replace them in the homes with new, and younger, servants. The older girls are then transformed into prostitutes, which increases the profits they earn for their captors—sex slavery. When they start delivering babies, this provides a new revenue stream, though the girls get nothing but tragedy. This is when they become breeder slaves, producing infants for sale.

The system is designed to strip these girls of their humanity. Breaking their spirits is a basic part of the business. To their captors they are nothing more than profitable animals meant to be used in every way possible, then tossed aside.

Though human traffickers have no love for babies, they love the profits babies can provide from couples who want to adopt them. Some of these infants are kept captive as they grow up. Kids are easy to control, and as we have seen they have many uses. The most attractive ones go to baby mills which quickly market them to couples who are willing to pay. These are the lucky ones who stay with their captors for only a short time before drawing the highest prices. The slave traders know that these babies are prized merchandise and treat them well while they have them. They are fed, clothed, and despite the lack of love, the care they receive is first class. Those who don't bring top dollar aren't as lucky. Their captors train them to go to work early, sometimes by the age of five. Some traffickers rent these abused children to farms and factories, while others sell them outright to new "owners."

This process creates a generational enslavement. An enslaved girl gives birth to an infant that's not attractive enough for immediate sale. Because these children are often living in cultures that value males far more than females, most of the rejected infants are girls. In such cultures a girl baby must be quite special to even draw a second look. Prospective buyers want male heirs, or, when they occasionally shop for a girl, they will want her to grow up to be a beautiful bride. To these parents, the only use for a girl is that of attracting prosperous suitors from good families.

The unwanted infant grows into childhood. Her captors rent her out to farmers, and she works long hours in the fields. When she's old enough, she's forced down the same path as her mother, and must become a prostitute. Soon she has her own less-than-perfect infant, and the cycle repeats.

This is how it works in the world's poorest regions, where whole populations live in desperate poverty. Most of these babies are sold in neighboring countries, or within their own borders, but some of them find their way to the United States.

As we've seen, not all captured babies become slaves. Some of the luckier children are sold to parents who give them good lives. This might sound like the dark cloud's silver lining, but that ignores the family left behind. Though some desperately poor parents can be coerced into selling their children, many attractive infants from working families are kidnapped, and sold to American buyers. Many of these buyers are agents with the resources to create proper documentation. These agents then list the babies with "legal" adoption agencies. The agencies help prospective parents find the child of their dreams. They then provide additional legal documentation, assuring parents that the process is within the law.

Subash was the first son of Sivagama and her husband, Nageshwar Rao. They lived in a village in Southern India where Nageshwar painted newly constructed homes and buildings for a living. Though the couple was far from rich, they worked hard, and had what they needed to raise a family. By the standards of the area they were doing well.

Like most villages, theirs had a pump where residents went to get their water. Like most of the other village women, Sivagama walked to the well every day. Within sight of the pump were several small businesses where she bought other essentials and did her daily errands. Though the pump was in the middle of a busy area with a lot of foot traffic, most of the passersby lived nearby. Sivagama usually knew almost everyone she saw. The culture she inhabited was like those which produced the saying: "It takes a village to raise a child." Sivagama looked about, saw the faces of friends and neighbors, and thought nothing of leaving her small son for just a few moments in a secure spot by the well. She knew he wouldn't be out of her sight for more than a minute, but that was all it took. When she glanced at the place where she'd left him, Subash was gone.

Police later theorized that a man probably spirited Subash away in a three-wheeled auto rickshaw. In the years that followed, investigators would learn that the boy changed hands again the very next day. That's when a nearby orphanage paid a good price for him. As Subash's parents, family, and friends scoured the entire state of Tamil searching for their lost son, the baby grew into a little boy there at the orphanage. Two years later he was a healthy, good-natured, light-skinned toddler—a good candidate for adoption in many Western nations.

Eventually investigators would show that this potential marketability was the perpetrators' motive for the kidnapping. The orphanage paid Subash's kidnappers about $236 for the boy. They created fictional documentation, making up details about his birth mother and place of origin. Because he was healthy, he wouldn't be a huge drain on their resources, and with one more child in their care they could get more subsidies. As legal guardian to Subash, and many others like him, the orphanage received funds from charities and the government. These subsidies guaranteed that the child's upkeep was paid, even before he or she was sold. That meant when they finally found a family who wanted Subash, the price he brought was virtually all profit. The orphanage was doing this with many children, and their average fee was about $3,500. Over a twelve-year period the orphanage did this with at least 165 babies.

A decade later Scott Carney, an American reporter for *Mother Jones* magazine, began connecting the dots in Subash's story. Carney traced a line from village to orphanage to American adoption agency, and finally to a middle-income Midwestern family. There he found a boy just entering his teens living in a family that had adopted two other children from India. Though the parents had heard news reports about adoption irregularities, they'd managed to put the stories out of their minds. How could they do otherwise? They'd already brought these kids into their family, loving and nurturing them from very young ages. Today Subash and his siblings are American kids. America is the only home they remember. When speaking of Subash, his alarmed adoptive mother told Carney: "To him, India does not exist."

Subash's parents in India were surprisingly understanding when they learned of their son's fate. They didn't want to tear him away from the only world he knows. Instead Subash's Indian parents have reached out to his American family, giving his adoptive parents assurances that all they want is his happiness. However, at last report, members of Subash's American family have declined to respond.

Subash is one of many thousands of pawns in this kind of human trafficking. Kidnapping attractive infants for sale to Westerners holds the promise of big payoffs all along the line. The kidnappers got about $236 for a single day's work—this in an area where a well-paid worker makes barely $5 per day. As previously noted, the orphanage broke even on his upkeep, then probably saw a profit of about $3,500 on the sale. The adoption agency paid for his journey to the States, but they were rewarded handsomely by his American parents. The final total of all these transactions was well over $20,000.

In the seventeen years since Subash was abducted, stealing babies for sale to Westerners has become more and more of an international problem. It's a common crime in the more impoverished parts of India and China, but in the world's poorest nations, trafficking is often a basic support for the economy.

Zimbabwean journalist, Problem Masau, has reported on this issue from Zimbabwe's neighbor, the East African nation of Malawi. He went to Karonga, a township on Lake Nyasa, near the country's northern border with Tanzania. Like many African townships,

Karonga is a collection of villages. The township's hub and business center are on the Lake. Scattered around it are several small farming and fishing villages. Each has a few huts surrounded by fields under cultivation.

Archeologists regard this part of Africa as a possible birthplace of the world's first human societies, and their excavations have turned up ancient tools from its earth. But the township's more recent history is dominated by human dislocation and trafficking. The township was founded in 1877 as a hub of the Arab slave trade, which still thrived before Westerners arrived. European pioneers introduced their own labor systems which weren't so different from slavery. Native peoples labored, while their European bosses took the profits. Not quite two decades later, in 1895, the British bought the outpost, ending out-and-out sales of human beings. However transporting natives for involuntary work didn't end. Many villagers learned that being subjects to the Crown left them open to being taken from their homes to remote plantations.

There they would work in tobacco and tea fields, often until they died. This colonial labor system decimated villages all over Africa.

Now, in 2016, Problem Masau was seeing a similar form of wholesale human trafficking. Again, local communities bore its scars. The children he met in Karonga were either very thin, or had bellies distended from their lack of nourishment. Some went to nearby schools for a time, while others never bothered. In their society when a child is old enough to work, the fields become schools. Kids learn to plant, tend, and reap as soon as they are physically ready. Traditionally these are the skills that matter.

When Tanzanian traffickers cross the border and start talking of high wages and less working hours, these children listen. "Strange people from Tanzania come here, promising our children manna from heaven," sixty-three-year-old Enock Mutinje told Masau. "Often the young boys and girls are tempted, and a few have disappeared. We never heard from them again." Mutinje has lived in Karonga his entire life.

When Mutinje was born, Malawi and Tanzania were still ruled by Britain, and villages near the present-day border were even more remote. The Arab slave trade had ended decades earlier, and roads into the region had fallen into disrepair. This was one moment when Karonga was relatively free of human traffickers. It was simply too hard to reach. That took the profit out of trafficking. This situation ended when Malawi gained its independence in the 1960s. That was when the government of President Hastings Banda built the M-1, a modern road stretching from the country's northern border to its southernmost provinces. Highways brought cars, trucks, and busses, greatly easing the task of trading human beings.

In 2016 several human trafficking cases involving Malawian children came to light. In an incident in July a truck crammed with fifty-seven children managed to get past border authorities in Zimbabwe and

Mozambique. It wasn't until they reached the South African border that customs inspectors got suspicious. The driver managed to get back in the truck and make a run for it, but South African police stopped the vehicle a few minutes later. They opened the back of the truck, and two hungry, overheated kids fell onto the ground. More spilled out after them. "[T]hese children were being transported as if they were goats," said Kgomotso Phahlane, South Africa's acting National Police Commissioner.

The human trafficking problem Masau wrote about is rooted in the economic troubles that plague the entire region. He spoke to Reverend Zacc Kawalala, chairman of the Ethics, Peace and Justice Commission of the Evangelical Association of Malawi. Kawalala hopes to see policies and programs that would target the problem's real cause: the dire poverty that defines these villages. "Governments should seriously consider implementing pro-poor and sustainable policies and programs that add value to the economy… rather than opting for short-term politically motivated policies and programs that do not add any value." Kawalala added that these programs must address "extreme poverty and unemployment in general."

Even with this larger problem of wholesale trafficking, Malawi and its neighbors aren't free from the controversies over the adoption methods of Westerners. Prized babies can bring high prices on the black market. Up until recently Malawi's laws only covered domestic adoptions—those where Malawian parents adopt Malawian children. There were no regulations whatsoever covering international adoptions.

Malawi is the place of origin for one of the most famous instances of international adoption. This began during a visit by the pop superstar, Madonna. She adopted two Malawian children. The first was a boy named David Banda (no relation to Malawi's former president, Hastings Banda). Madonna and her then-husband, film director Guy Ritchie, adopted David after a visit to Malawi in 2006. Though the adoption process seemed reasonably transparent at the time, it also revealed how some developing countries tacitly encourage adoption-for-profit through their lax adoption laws. During an interview on Oprah, Madonna said: "There are no [foreign] adoption laws in Malawi." At the time it was true.

Madonna went on to adopt David's sister, Mercy, in 2009. It was reported that she had compensated the family, promising in both cases to give these kids all the advantages of Western education, healthcare, and nutrition. In this she has been true to her word. But the children's uncle, Peter Banet, claims that Madonna has reneged on other pledges. He claims that she also promised to return to the family's village so that the children could maintain contact with their blood relatives. Though Madonna and David have returned to Malawi several times, according to Banet, they've never contacted the family.

At this writing the singer has applied to a Malawian court to adopt David and Mercy's younger siblings who are twin sisters. Mr. Banet is opposed to the idea. He has told the twins' immediate family: "You may never see your children again, never have contact with them. It will be as if your children have died. That is the pain we feel every day." Speaking of the earlier adoptions, he says: "I put my hand up in court, swore an oath and signed the adoption consent. I can never forgive myself for that, and there is sadness and disappointment throughout my family. I must take the blame. I am ashamed."

David and Mercy are examples of gray areas that often complicate the issue of human trafficking. Are Westerners helping these children? Or tearing them away from their proper families? Are impoverished parents right to give up their children to those who can provide them with the "advantages" of a Western lifestyle? Are the traditions we prize better than their native customs?

Every case is different, and news reports leave out far more than they include. We can never know all the variables that go into these decisions. But when the children come, piled high in hot trucks like loads of cargo, and when their reward is long hours of labor in fields or factories, the wrongdoing is clear. In such cases the only just path is that of ending slavery. If we can finally right that wrong, we might do a better job of bringing the gray areas into focus.

SLAVES IN THE FAMILY

"Chains do not hold a marriage together."

-Simone Signoret

Though forced marriages rarely end in lifelong happiness, they are the norm throughout much of the world. In many societies, women are customarily sold into marriage by their families. These families can usually cite religious and/or ethnic reasons with roots in distant eras distorted by memory and legend. Often the practice of forced marriage is supported by traditions going back hundreds, and even thousands, of years. It's present in folk tales, legends, and even in the Bible. Some immigrants carry this tradition from their homeland, trying desperately to preserve it in the freer societies where they settle. This encourages the spread of slavery through forced marriage far beyond the borders of individual nations or cultures. In the last few decades it has grown into one of the most common, yet damaging forms of human trafficking.

Even in a world where freedom and equality have become almost universal ideals, some cultures still fail to give women the same respect as men. In many families the birth of a girl is seen as a curse, rather than a cause for celebration. Though most nations' laws have changed, allowing women the same rights as men, customs and traditions have not yet caught up with these new and legal freedoms. Many communities still hold to traditions that limit women. These traditions involve various restrictions, sometimes not allowing women to work, or own property, or gain education. Often these women never learn to read and are denied information about their rights. Women who try to open businesses, or work in professions, find themselves marginalized, ostracized, and boycotted. A girl who can't find a husband is regarded as a drain on her family's resources. Many poor families don't even wait for their daughters to reach marriageable age. If a man offers money, they take it, and give him the girl he wants.

This is another of the types of human trafficking where many cases fall into a gray area. Parents who practice this tradition seldom see it as slavery. They will point out examples of the custom that have resulted in happy, prosperous unions. To be fair, not all traditional arranged marriages should be seen as "forced." In societies with these traditions many women believe in arranging their children's marriages. Often the tradition calls for mothers and other female relatives to do the arranging. They see it as one role where they have an advantage over their husbands. Nonetheless, some of these women are unwittingly selling their daughters into permanent enslavement.

According to the website of the AHA Foundation (named for activist/author Ayaan Hirsi Ali): "A forced marriage occurs when an individual is forced to enter into a marriage against her will and without her consent. A forced marriage differs from an arranged marriage, in which families arrange meetings between children in the hopes of fostering a voluntary relationship that will lead to marriage." The post goes on to describe how families arrange the first meeting between a boy and girl, with marriage being the obvious (but not inevitable) goal. "[T]he ultimate decision to marry remains with the couple."

But many "arranged" marriages ignore these rules and cross the boundary into "forced." Often the woman is coerced by various combinations of indoctrination, threats, and money. In such a situation the woman must marry the man, essentially becoming his slave. There's no choice here. If she resists, she's subjected to extortion, and possibly honor violence and death. Honor violence and honor killing are the abuse and/or murder of a girl because she has brought dishonor upon her family by refusing to give in to a forced marriage.

The Human Trafficking Center estimates that about 140 million women and girls will be forced into marriages against their will in the decade ending in 2020. Each day that means thirty-nine thousand women are entering lives which the UN has labeled: "a contemporary form of slavery."

Though Americans tend to see this as a problem that only happens in foreign countries, the practice does have direct effects here in the United States. Many young students come to the U.S. from those countries to attend our schools. When these children reach a certain age (often quite young by our standards) their families use coercion (threats of ostracism and violence) to force these girls (and occasionally boys) to abandon their studies and come home to marry a stranger. Thousands of these female students are then removed from their American schools, brought home, and forced to either marry, or suffer shame, abuse, and sometimes even death. According to the AHA website: "Once married, victims' experience includes increased rates of infant and maternal mortality, rape, domestic violence and suicide. The coercion, exploitation and ongoing violence involved in these scenarios mirrors the key traits of human trafficking."

America's experience with forced marriage isn't limited to foreign students who get summoned back to their own countries. It happens among people who are born and raised here. In some isolated communities it's a common practice. One recent study uncovered about fifteen hundred of these marriages taking place in America every year. Most experts believe the number is far higher.

In 2016 PBS aired a story of two women who had escaped forced marriages.

Nina grew up in what was considered, by the standards of their Michigan township, to be a normal family. They lived outside of town on a forty-acre farm. Just about everyone she'd ever known was a part of their conservative Evangelical community. She hardly got any day-to-day exposure to news or social media. That meant a life of prayer, conformity, and avoiding most social contacts with outsiders. Nina wasn't physically abused or held there by force. After all, this was the family she'd been born into; but under the circumstances she'd had little chance to learn about any alternatives.

Though Nina and her older sister knew their day was coming, when that day finally dawned, she was surprised. She wrote in her diary: "This morning after breakfast Papa sat [us] down at the kitchen table and nailed us with a load of bricks. He believes he has found husbands for both of us." Nina hadn't expected this so soon. She had assumed that since her sister was older, their parents would find a husband for the older girl first, giving Nina more time. Nonetheless she went through with it. She had no real understanding that there might be some other way.

Nina was nineteen years old. She was under no legal obligation to marry this man, but she also couldn't comprehend the difference between obligations under the law, and those covering family connections. All her life she'd been taught that this would happen. Overt coercion wasn't necessary. After all, her sister was going along with it, so why should

Nina be different? If she felt something like discomfort, she managed to overcome that on her wedding day. She wore the white dress, said the vows, and cut the cake. Even now she says: "It didn't feel 'forced.'"

For a decade she lived with the man her parents had chosen. She shared his bed, bore his children, and did all that was expected of a traditional, obedient wife. But each year the psychological pressures grew. With each meal, each prayer, and each intimacy she felt more and more like a prisoner. As her need for freedom grew, the pressures to stay intensified. Everyone around her was a part of this pressure. Her awareness of the consequences preyed on her mind. To leave him, she would have to leave everything: parents, friends, church, and community—the only world she knew. Despite all that the day finally came when, as she puts it: "Staying was more frightening than leaving."

Many of us are amazed at such stories. We live in a world where most of us begin the process of separation from our homes at an early age. We go to school filled with students who come from a variety of backgrounds. Often, we see "different" lives right next door. Our cultures clash daily, and parents struggle to teach their children the standards of their own lives and homes, while balancing home life with the public life that happens outside the front door. This isn't an easy task for parents, but it's necessary if we are to live in a free society.

Most of us think of forced marriage as something that could only happen in the remote isolation of the countryside, as it did in the rural community where Nina grew up. But urban communities also find ways to seal themselves off from the outside. They too are motivated by cultural and religious traditions, though these are sometimes joined by fear, and even harsh hostility toward any outsiders.

Another nineteen-year-old named Fraidy Reiss grew up in an ultra-Orthodox Jewish community not far from New York City. Though we hardly think of that region as "isolated," Fraidy's family kept within the confines of their congregation. Arranged marriages were the norm here, and as Fraidy reached marriageable age, she says: "I felt I had no choice." Things started out well, and Reiss describes her wedding ceremony as "joyous." However, once she moved in with her new husband, her joy quickly turned sour.

The husband her parents had chosen for her was an abuser who terrorized his new bride. The torture started almost immediately, and soon escalated into death threats. "He would describe how he was going to kill me in detail," she told her PBS interviewer, "how I was going to take my last breath." Though it took her several years, and the births of two children, she finally broke away.

Fraidy knew that in leaving her husband she was also leaving her entire past life. Her family and friends saw divorce as sinful and would no longer have anything to do with her. In 2010 she got a restraining order against her husband which is still in force seven years later. She still shares custody of their children with him, but the circumstances governing contact between the former spouses are strictly defined and designed for her protection.

After Nina's break with her husband, she moved to a small city nearby, taking their children. What little contact she has with her former husband is the only connection left between her and her former community. Her family has severed all ties with her. Over time she has built up a new network of support among friends who live near her new home. She tells an interviewer that: "Freedom gave me peace."

Fraidy notes that few people have the strength, vision, or courage to successfully break away. As she began her path to divorce and independence, she had no idea where to turn. That inspired her to start her own organization to bring hope and connection to other women who are breaking free from this kind of slavery. She notes that a part of the problem stems from embarrassment and shame. Though these women might be entering a world where they can find support, all their upbringing, and all that they hear from their families as they leave, tells them that they are wrong, and that they are taking the path of sin. "It's so important to talk about this publicly," she says. She calls her group: "Unchained at Last."

The "Unchained at Last" website puts a spotlight on this hidden terror. It notes that some American victims of forced marriage are as young as twelve. The site serves as a connection for women who live in the isolation of this type of slavery. It also promotes activism aimed at ending the practice. Legislatures in several states, including California, Massachusetts, and Pennsylvania have passed, or are considering new legislative remedies.

The United Kingdom has seen even more of this human disaster. Great Britain's strong connection with its former colonies means more people arriving on its shores who come from cultures where such slavery is ignored, or even condoned. England, Whales, and Northern Ireland have passed ever stricter laws against forced marriage, but there is still much to be done. Though twelve hundred new cases come to light each year, in the first year after passing an anti-trafficking statute only one violator had been prosecuted. That's why there are cases like those of a girl named Jasmine.

Jasmine (who prefers not to use her real name) is from London, but she was born in a South Asian country that was once a British colony. When she was three years old her parents moved the family to England. Except for a couple of brief trips back to Asia when she was young, Jasmine grew up knowing only life in twenty-first-century Britain. Then, after ten years, her parents decided she should spend her summer holiday with relatives. She looked forward to the journey. She wanted to see her parents' homeland through the lens of her growing maturity.

"I just thought it was a normal family holiday," she told a reporter later, "but on the last day, ten minutes before we left to go back to the airport, my [uncles and aunts] came around with sweets and money. They kept asking me if I liked my cousin, who was five years older and lived out there. I thought: 'He's my cousin; I don't think of him that way.'"

It took some time for Jasmine to understand the meaning of all this. As she thought about what had happened, it slowly dawned on her: the family had brought the sweets and money as offerings to the young girl they thought of as their son's future bride. To them this was a celebration. As far as they were concerned it was now inevitable that she and her cousin would marry as soon as Jasmine turned eighteen.

Jasmine flew home, wondering how all this could happen. She liked her cousin, but the idea of him as a boyfriend was totally foreign to her. And why would she even consider marrying such a man? Obviously marrying him would mean moving away from Britain. For Jasmine that was unthinkable. To her, London was home. When she arrived in London, she quickly realized that her parents were on board with this plan. Soon they were expecting her to talk to her cousin regularly on the phone. Often his parents came on the line "asking me stuff that I hadn't even spoken to my mum about. It was awkward," she said later.

In London Jasmine felt as if she was a normal thirteen-year-old except for one thing: she was already "engaged" to a man who lived on the other side of the world. Through her early teens her parents regularly reminded her of this. The pressure began with words, but it quickly escalated. "My mum used to hit me, slap me, and pull my hair," Jasmine recalled. Her parents made it clear that this marriage was an absolute requirement. Soon they began taunting her for adopting Western ways. They forbade her to go anywhere if boys might be present, and soon they were putting strict limits on the time she could spend with her girlfriends.

As the conflict intensified, her parents' pressure and violence increased. At one point her mother nearly strangled her, and both of her parents made it clear that any resistance would bring dishonor and shame to their family. They sent her back to their home country for another "holiday" visit, but in truth it was simply their attempt to cement the bonds that would inevitably lead to marriage. From their side it seemed to work. When she returned home her unwanted fiancé called more and more often. If he was enthusiastic, how could their plan fail?

When Jasmine took the GCSE tests (General Certificate of Secondary Education—the British Commonwealth's main measure of qualifications for higher education) she wondered why she was bothering. "What's the point if they want me to get married?" she said to herself. Unable to focus on her studies, she failed. Her parents hardly seemed to care. After all, why would a girl who was going to get married worry about higher education? As far as they were concerned, the only thing she needed to know was how to be a good wife. Then, as she approached fifteen, Jasmine found a boyfriend there in London. She kept it secret, but gossip filtered back to her parents that their daughter was running around with boys.

Alarmed by this development, her parents told her to finish up any schoolwork fast; she would be leaving for Asia the following week. When Jasmine claimed that her life was her own, her comment drew verbal and physical rebukes from her parents. "It's not your life," her mother shouted as she slapped Jasmine.

When Jasmine returned for her last classes, she told one of her teachers what was happening. The teacher helped her contact the police and social services. The police were helpful, assessing Jasmine as an "acute risk," but her social worker saw things differently. This woman tried to persuade Jasmine to move home. Though this advice violated all department guidelines for cases of forced marriage, the social worker continued her efforts, tricking Jasmine into attending a meeting where her parents were present. They'd arrived, ready to take their daughter home. The social worker told Jasmine everything would be all right, that her parents hadn't understood the depth of her opposition to the marriage. She promised that they would not force the issue. She told Jasmine to go home with them and "act normal." Jasmine refused.

Knowing that she couldn't rely on any help from social services, Jasmine stayed with friends. Her parents soon tracked her down and began calling her constantly. They lied, saying her mother was sick in the hospital. When this didn't work, they tried other ploys. Jasmine began leaving her parents' voicemails and emails unanswered. They responded by posting their emails from new addresses with innocuous subject lines. Whenever she opened one, and recognized what it was, she deleted it. Despite her efforts they refused to give in. Their harassment continued for months.

When the police learned that the social worker hadn't done anything to stop this, they stepped in. They soon found Jasmine a place to stay in another city. Finally, a court gave her what the British call a "Forced Marriage Protection Order." Now Jasmine is safe and finishing her studies. Her local social services unit claimed they hadn't been aware that the proposed marriage was a forced one. They said Jasmine's social worker had been acting according to the guidelines for an "arranged" marriage.

This demonstrates two aspects of this problem: the attitudes of local social service authorities, and how, in practice, the line between "forced" and "arranged" unions gets blurred. In both Britain and America, social service agencies write their guidelines with the unity of families uppermost in their minds. One of their first principles is that of helping families remain close, both emotionally and physically. Unless there is a compelling case for separation, the default policy always favors this concept of children staying with their families until they reach adulthood. In most cases this makes sense, but on this issue, and in these circumstances, a girl's family can become her enemy.

If Jasmine had been raised in the confines of the culture of her birthplace perhaps, she would have accepted her parents' decrees in a docile manner. Maybe force would not have been necessary, and Jasmine might have gone along with the whole "arrangement." But her parents had raised her in London, allowing her to be educated and socialized in Western ways. Though she'd grown up knowing more and more freedom, now they wanted her to accept the life of a slave. When the conflict escalated, they were ready and willing to use violence and coercion to force her into a marriage she didn't want. In their home country she would have been one more girl to be bartered for money and social position. In England she'd grown up with the vision of being a free young woman with an innate right to choose her own relationships. British law recognized that choice, allowing her to escape from her parents' grasp.

"Slavery" means different things in different parts of the world. In many societies arranged marriages aren't seen as enslavement. Wherever we are born, we are formed not only by our families, but by the societies, attitudes, and conditions around us. When a child has been brought up with the promise of freedom, forced marriage is unjust. In truly free societies it is also regarded as immoral, and illegal. Jasmine, and other women like her, cannot be forced to remain chained to their parents' ideas. They have the right to choose their own paths and live their own lives.

Forced Work, Forced Sex, and Forced Smuggling

"Her body was a prison; her mind was a prison...
even the sky felt like a prison."

-Ann Brashares

ix long picnic tables are lined with expectant
people. These are needy souls whose lives
straddle the nearby border between Arizona and
Mexico. They arrive hungry. Theirs are the faces of
dashed hopes and damaged dreams. They left the
poverty of their lives in Mexico hoping that their labor
would earn them better wages in the United States.
They've paid what little money they could get to
"coyotes," whose specialty is transporting across the
border. These coyotes make promises on one side, then
break them as soon as they have their human cargo in
the U.S. Victims wind up as forced laborers on farms,
in factories, and in brothels. Some make trouble, some
escape, and others are cast off to try life on their own in
a hostile country. At some point any of these "illegals"
might get caught by American authorities. That's when
they get deported back into Mexico. The luckier ones
might wind up at these tables.

The tables and food are a part of the Kino Border Initiative. This particular Kino venture is dedicated to feeding those who've been deported from the States back into Mexico. Directing a small battalion of volunteers, two Jesuit priests make sure everyone gets their fill of corn, beans, and pork rinds.

Father Machuca grips a microphone, as he gives advice to these new deportees for their next attempt at crossing. He must assume they will all try again, and he wants them to have a fighting chance. Some of it sounds a lot like what parents tell their children, but most of Father Machuca's listeners are in their teens and twenties—old enough to understand the full implications of what the priest is saying. Don't accept rides from border-bound strangers who promise a better life, he tells them. You can count yourself lucky if such a ride results only in some verbal abuse, and a quick trip back. Often there are far worse consequences. Don't accept the offer of a cell phone to contact other family members. Many captors will make a note of the number so that they can contact these same relatives with threats and demands, telling them they must pay to guarantee your safety.

Machuca's American partner in this effort is Father Sean Carroll. He tells a reporter: "The vulnerability is very high here. [The coyotes] want to contract the migrants to try to cross again." Most coyotes work for immediate payments, but a lot of their employers have a different business model. These employers are members of Mexico's drug cartels. They hire coyotes to trick these migrants into carrying large quantities of drugs to their distributors here in the States; once a migrant worker has performed this function, her or she is often abandoned, or even murdered.

In Tucson, Arizona, about sixty miles north of Nogales, Juanita Molina runs two groups dedicated to easing the plight of these migrants: Border Action Network and Humane Borders. She, and other workers, place water tanks in desert locations selected based on where victims of dehydration are most often found. Many illegals die of thirst before they reach their destinations. Molina and her allies also argue for more humane treatment of migrants by our Border Patrol.

"We feed the danger by forcing all of these people into the shadows," Molina told one interviewer. She notes that the Border Patrol's strategy is to make crossing more difficult. To do this they shut off all easy routes, which funnels crossers onto more risky paths. She wonders if the Patrol understands that this leads to greater danger, and more deaths. "It's hard to know," she says. But one thing she has seen is the actual damage: severely dehydrated crossers, and too many corpses far from the roads into towns. "The dynamic of pushing people further into these wilderness areas is almost like putting out meat for the wolves," she said.

The statistics are often staggering. One human rights group, the Washington Office on Latin America, counts over four hundred migrant deaths per year. This number doesn't change much, even when the pool of crossers goes down. In 2005 the organization counted 492 migrant deaths. By 2012 the total number of people crossing was down by two-thirds, but 463 of those who attempted it were found dead.

Over fifty thousand unwitting victims are trafficked into the U.S. every year. That's not the number of migrants coming here. They fit into a category of human enslavement all their own, with much higher numbers of victims. Their plight is more predictable, but no less abusive and humiliating. Most migrants are simply farmworkers who will be underpaid, overworked, then finally released. Most of these find their way back to Mexico. Some are deported, while others go on their own. The ones who are trafficked are usually girls, young women, or sometimes children of both sexes. Over fifteen thousand per year are brought in from Mexico and Central America. Almost all are used as prostitutes, then discarded onto the streets.

One recent report from the Dallas Women's Foundation in Texas cited "740 girls under the age of 18" being marketed for sex in that state during a thirty-day period. "712 of these girls were being marketed through Internet classified web sites," the Foundation reported. "Twenty-eight were being marketed through escort services."

Here in the U.S. we tend to see this problem only in terms of our borders, but that's just one part of the crisis of human trafficking. As we've already seen, human traffickers often do business within their own country's territory. Americans are trafficked to American buyers, and most human trafficking victims in Mexico suffer these assaults and indignities without ever leaving their country.

Numbers begin by horrifying us, but as the human toll mounts, the statistics soon become numbing. To see the problem up close, we can look at the case of Karla Jacinto. When a CNN reporter interviewed this brave young victim, Karla focused her listeners on only one number: 43,200. To reach this figure she multiplied thirty times per day by seven days per week, then calculated what that would come to over four years. 43,200—it's the number of times men raped her when she was held captive by human traffickers.

Karla was a victim of a human trafficking system with tentacles reaching to New York, San Francisco, and every other major American city. Those are some of the most obvious destinations for human trafficking victims, but CNN was asking where these victims came from. What they found was that just a few small Mexican towns serve as launching points for most of these trafficking operations, shipping some victims north, while sending others to cities in Mexico. One of the most prominent of these towns is Tenancingo in Central Mexico.

Though Tenancingo is home to only thirteen thousand people, it serves as one of North America's most lucrative sources of human trafficking. It's a haven for pimps, and a training ground for girls who are just waking up to the fact that they're trapped in a life of prostitution. According to Susan Coppedge, our State Department's Ambassador at Large to Combat Human Trafficking, "That's what the town does... yet in smaller, rural communities the young girls don't have any idea [about] the town's reputation, so they are not suspicious..."

Long before Karla's 43,200 rapes began, she had suffered from sexual abuse in her home. It had started at the age of five. "I came from a dysfunctional family," she told CNN. "I was sexually abused and mistreated [by] a relative." Then came the young man who uttered kind words and drove a fast car. Twelve-year-old Karla was waiting for friends near a subway stop in Mexico City. She barely noticed the little boy selling candies until he approached her. He held out a candy, saying it was a gift.

Even in Mexico's most impoverished regions, a stranger offering candy is suspect. But this was delivered by a little boy. This seemingly innocent child then introduced Karla to a fast-talking, seemingly compassionate man. The man immediately disarmed her by recognizing her suspicions and revealing his own vulnerabilities. He'd had a difficult childhood, he said; then when he asked about her own upbringing, she hinted at the abuse she'd suffered. Of course, the man had endured similar abuse. He was a sympathetic fellow victim . . . or that's what he told her.

In that initial contact the man was a perfect gentleman. The two exchanged phone numbers, and a week later he called. When he invited her to visit a nearby town with him, she accepted. When he showed up in a Firebird Trans Am, she got excited. Perhaps this man was truly her ticket to a better life. "It was exciting for me," she said. "He asked me to get in the car to go places."

He didn't try to take her right there and then. Instead he waited until a night when Karla got home a little late. Her mother had locked the door, leaving Karla to fend for herself until morning. That day Karla went with the man. She lived with him for the next three months. He had affectionate sex with her and showered her with gifts. "Everything was beautiful," Karla recalled much later.

In the years to come, Karla would look back and see that the red flags had already been there. Sometimes her new boyfriend would leave her by herself in the apartment for days at a time. He had cousins who came by every week, always with new girls whom she would never see again. As she watched these girls appear, then vanish, her suspicions began. Finally, she got up the nerve to ask what business his cousins were in. "They're pimps," he told her, in a tone that implied she would have a role in this, too. "A few days later he started telling me everything I had to do." He spoke of positions, services, rates, and charges. He told her "the things I had to do with the client and for how long, how I was to treat them and how I had to talk to them so that they would give me more money."

For the next four years Karla had to prostitute herself to as many men as possible. They started her in Guadalajara, one of Mexico's biggest cities. She did what she was told, but it was often too much for her. "Some men would laugh at me because I was crying. I had to close my eyes so that I wouldn't see what they were doing to me, so that I wouldn't feel anything," she told CNN.

Other cities followed. Karla had to work in brothels, motels, private homes, and sometimes they sent her out to walk the streets looking for johns. Once they had her trained, the pace was relentless, brutal, and sometimes bloody: thirty customers per day, seven days per week. When one of her johns left her with a visible hickey, her pimp "corrected" her violently. "He started beating me with a chain in all of my body. He punched me... kicked me, pulled my hair, spit in [my] face, and... burned me with the iron."

One day police raided the hotel where she was working, but what seemed like a rescue turned out to be nothing of the kind. The police separated the girls into groups, put them in different rooms, then forced them into compromising positions while videotaping them. The officers told the girls that they must do whatever they were told, or these tapes would be shown to the girls' families.

"They knew we were minors," she told her interviewer. "We were not even developed... There were girls who were only ten years old. There were girls who were crying. They told the officers they were minors, and nobody paid attention."

Then came something that should've been a blessing, but for Karla it was a nightmare. She got pregnant. The father was Karla's pimp. At fifteen she gave birth to a baby girl. To Karla this was simply one more tragic chapter. Her daughter was born a slave, and unless Karla could escape with her, this child would grow up in this world. From the start the girl's father regularly threatened her with beatings, torture, and worse, all to cement his control of Karla.

Two years after her daughter's birth, Karla was finally freed. Her pimp was arrested during an anti-trafficking operation, and the physical torture was over. She's now twenty-three, and every day she must live with the lingering effects of pain and terror. Instead of succumbing to the sadness, Karla has become an advocate against human trafficking. She's brought her evidence to the attention of Pope Francis and testified before Congress in support of Megan's Law. Her story was a part of the fuel for this vital legislation that tightens the screws on human traffickers.

Karla wants us all to be aware of this growing crisis around the world. "These minors are being abducted, lured, and yanked away from their families," she says. "Don't just listen to me. You need to learn about what happened to me and take the blindfold off your eyes."

She always comes back to that one statistic, the one that is hers alone: 43,200 rapes. How can we ignore her?

Most human trafficking victims are young people who want the same things we all want: the opportunity to improve their lives. Far too many find only abuse, torture, and enslavement. No matter where they suffer, we must open our eyes, and demand that our leaders recognize the plight of these victims and take action to end it.

BODY PARTS

"I am the slave and ruler of my own body and I wish to do with it exactly as I please."

Charlotte Eriksson

I n the Chinese province of Shanxi a six-year-old boy named Binbin went missing from his family. His parents had last seen him playing outside their home. A few hours later they found him lying in a field, crying. "[He] had blood all over his face," his distraught father told a reporter. "We thought he had fallen down and smashed his face."

It wasn't until Binbin had been rushed to the hospital that his parents learned the grisly truth. Someone had gouged out the little boy's eyes. Police searched the area near where he'd been found. They found both eyes with the corneas carefully removed. Binbin had been a victim of a relatively new form of human trafficking: that of stealing people's healthy organs for transplant into patients desperate for life and health.

In the United States alone well over one hundred thousand people are waiting for an organ donation on any given day. Most of these patients are running a race with death. Some of them will be on a waiting list for years, hoping the right organ will turn up. Their feelings about donors vary, but it's a complex emotional mix. Of course, they will be thankful, yet, in many cases (and always with donated hearts) they're hoping and praying for an outcome that can only come when someone else dies.

Many of these patients lose the race, dying before an organ is available. Eighteen Americans die every day for want of a healthy organ. One healthy donor might save up to eight lives. Some patients are wealthy, and some doctors don't ask many questions when an organ arrives. This makes the illegal organ market hugely profitable. Profits draw criminals the way a light attracts moths. Once transplants became common, the rise of the black market in healthy organs became inevitable.

Breaking into this market isn't easy. To stay healthy an organ must have fresh blood and oxygen right up to the moment of harvest. In any legitimate setting a partial pancreas, intestine, lung, or liver can be taken from a living person and transplanted into the sick patient. If the donation is that of a whole vital organ like a heart, the donor must be declared brain dead, while oxygen and blood are provided by artificial means.

As anyone might guess, doing this illegally requires multiple participants. A healthy donor must be identified. This donor must then be either incapacitated (if he or she is expected to survive) or killed. Someone must have the expertise, tools, and equipment to remove and properly preserve the organ, then someone must be willing to buy it.

The true source of the organ might be kept from the patient. Even the surgeon might be unaware or misled about where the organ came from. But in every case several people know the true source, or enough about the process to be implicated. This includes the one who harvests the organ, those who help with its preservation and transport, and whoever makes the actual purchase. Beyond these few people are others who might not have direct knowledge, but who have ample reason to be suspicious. These might include administrators, doctors, nurses, and sometimes even the patient. They might justify what they are doing with the lives that are saved, but this requires a willful ignorance of those lives that have been sacrificed.

Cases of human trafficking for the harvesting of vital organs can be broken into four categories:

1. Victims who are killed for their organs.
2. Victims who are forced or tricked into giving their organs.

3. Victims who agree to sell their organs but are cheated out of some or all the money due them.

4. People who receive treatments that may or may not be necessary, and, while they are unconscious, an organ is removed without their knowledge.

Most victims come from the poorest, most vulnerable groups: the homeless, the uneducated, and migrants. In many of the world's poorest nations needy villagers sell their organs for a few hundred dollars. Many are lured in by promises that the surgery will help them by resolving some physical issue. When the operation is over, they know their recovery will take time, but they are comforted by having more money than they ever dared hope for, and sometimes by the expectation of better health. The money seldom lasts as long as they'd hoped, and when it's gone, they must face a future with the same ailment they had before, minus an organ.

Another growing group of victims are children. There are those like Binbin, whose targeting may have been random, and then there are children who've been captured or sold into slavery. When such a child has outlived his or her usefulness, the captors know they can make one last big profit selling the murdered child's organs on the black market.

This market includes lungs, hearts, livers, corneas, and more, but the strongest demand is for kidneys. The World Health Organization (WHO) estimates that seven thousand kidneys a year are illegally sold worldwide. A wealthy buyer might pay as much as $200,000 for a healthy kidney, but the donor seldom gets more than a few thousand dollars. As is true with many legal and reputable activities, like stocks, mortgages, and service contracts, the biggest slice gets taken by the brokers—middlemen who often never even see the body parts that produce their profits.

Many surgeons, administrators, and brokers simply can't resist the lure of big money. The organization Organ Watch estimates the worldwide black market to be about fifteen thousand to twenty thousand illegal transplants per year, averaging more than one per hour. One broker in China went so far as to place an ad online with the headline: "Donate a kidney and buy a new iPad!" The broker went on to say that if everything went quickly and easily, the donor might receive as much as $4,000 in addition to the tablet. "Quickly" usually means less than ten days.

Horror stories are just as easy to find in North America. Twenty-three-year-old Antonio Medina, an undocumented worker from Central America, was passing through Mexico on his way to the U.S. when he met a fellow migrant who'd lost his wife to a gang that trafficked in human organs. "Gangsters took both of them," Medina told a reporter during an interview in Mexico. "They put [the husband and wife] in separate rooms. He heard his wife screaming. After he went in, he saw her on a table with her chest wide open and without her heart or kidney." Medina's acquaintance would've been killed but for the timely appearance of Mexican authorities, who were raiding this illegal "clinic."

Many Americans are surprised to learn that some criminals do the same thing right here in the States. If we stop to consider all the factors, how could it be otherwise? We live in a wealthy country. Organs illegally harvested elsewhere will find their way into our system simply because the money is here. But there may be other sources that are closer to home. Though we have tough rules and regulation governing organ donation, we have no shortage of criminals. As we've already seen, we also have a market of desperate patients, many of whom have money. But how are the organs procured in a modern health system?

One common method involves brokers and funeral homes. The funeral home director will help with forged consent forms, death certificates, and other paperwork. This works best with bodies that are bound for cremation. That way the evidence is automatically destroyed. The broker, or broker's agent, harvests the healthy organs, and then the body is burned.

Other illegal organs come from live victims who've agreed to sell a kidney, or some other body part they feel they can spare. These donors are usually poor, so their compensation is often not much more than that paid to victims in impoverished countries. Finally, some organs come from people who've been kidnapped specifically for organ harvesting. Instead of trying the risky ransom route, kidnappers look for a wealthy patient who'll pay almost anything to live and aren't about sources. The victims here are potential witnesses. Once they've served their purpose, their kidnappers don't intend to let them live.

In the U.S. this kind of trafficking is on the rise, but many cases go unsolved. In January 2013 Kendrick Johnson, a seventeen-year-old high school student in Georgia, was found dead. His corpse was rolled up in a mat in the school gym. Local authorities assumed his death was a freak accident. The coroner ruled that Kendrick had died of "positional asphyxia" caused by getting trapped upside down in a rolled-up mat.

His mother and father refused to accept the official verdict. On their request a court ordered that Kendrick's body be exhumed. The parents then paid for their own autopsy on their son's body. This produced startling revelations. According to the pathologist the cause of Kendrick's death was blunt trauma to the neck. In other words, he'd been assaulted, and it killed him. The other finding seemed to indicate an obvious motive. The young man's brain, heart, lungs, and liver were gone. The body cavity had been stuffed with newspaper.

The FBI investigated, and though they couldn't find enough evidence to put anyone on trial, they did tell Kendrick's parents that the first autopsy was flawed, and the second one was correct. With so many organs surgically removed, the official verdict seems ludicrous, yet it was not immediately revised. The family is still seeking more definitive answers in a civil suit.

There are too many cases like Kendrick's—dead bodies, missing organs, and no answers. In 2012 a fifty-one-year-old Pennsylvania man died in a Philadelphia hospital. Though no one disputed that his death was preceded by a potentially fatal lung ailment, his mother was shocked when she learned the condition his body was in when it arrived at the funeral home. The man's eyes, heart, brain, and pancreas had been taken out. The authorities told her that his organs had been donated for educational purposes. But there was no record that the man, or his family, had approved the "donation."

In 2014 an aspiring actor from Georgia took off for L.A. to seek work, fame, and fortune. As far as anyone knows, he didn't get past Death Valley. His body was found there minus eyes, heart, kidney, and other organs. The work was surgical, and the rest of his body was intact. Investigators contended that his organs may have been eaten by a wild animal. This would've required razor-sharp teeth, and an intelligent neatness seldom found in the animal world.

University of California Berkeley anthropologist Nancy Scheper-Hughes spent ten years on the trail of traffickers in human organs. Though she couldn't get enough proof for convictions, she found evidence that black market organs were being transplanted into patients in cities throughout the United States. In an interview she said: "People all over were telling me that they didn't have to go to a Third World hospital but could get [brokered organ transplants] done in New York, Philadelphia or Los Angeles, at top hospitals, with top surgeons." She had no idea if the surgeons had any direct knowledge about the donors, but after gathering her evidence, she made presentations to any medical professionals who would agree to see her. After one such meeting with surgeons in a well-regarded Philadelphia facility "they basically threw me out," Scheper-Hughes told one reporter.

This trafficking in human body parts is related to other enslavement practices both directly and indirectly. This brings the notion of "vicious cycle" to a whole new level. For some human trafficker's, organ harvesting is their standard solution to the problem of the enslaved child who has outgrown his or her usefulness. The same applies to many women who are no longer desirable enough to be profitable as prostitutes. Like an old car, when they are no longer doing what's expected of them, they're still good for parts.

Like so many modern miracles, those that emerge from medical research can be double-edged swords. Over a half-century ago, when transplants were new, they seemed like strange outliers in a weird future that seemed inexplicable. Yet how could we resist these advances? If a heart wore out, or a liver suffered irreversible damage, we saw that a new one could give us decades of healthy, happy life. Soon these operations became commonplace. Many of us have friends, relatives, or acquaintances who have benefited from these miraculous innovations.

Yet few of us want to think about the dark side. The only entity that can create, nurture, and give long-term maintenance to lungs, kidneys, and hearts is a functioning human body. That's the one thing none of us can live without. As long as that is true there will be profit in this brand of trafficking. It's the duty of each individual to look at decisions in this realm with a hard, objective eye. It's a lot to ask, but some of us may have to make the ultimate sacrifice so that poor-but-healthy innocents survive.

Ruined Lives: Slavery and Pornography

"If prostitution is the main act, porn is the dress rehearsal."

-Anonymous

The line between human trafficking and pornography is often so thin that it sometimes appears to be invisible. Virtually all child pornography involves human trafficking and forced labor. No child freely volunteers for such a task. Often the lines are intentionally blurred so that the pornographer can claim to be working with "adults" who have taken the job freely. These are just two of the factors in play as investigators of these cases sort out what's moral and immoral, and right and wrong, and ultimately legal or illegal.

That's what investigators were doing when they started looking into a certain West Coast minister. Because his case has not yet been decided in the courts, we will call him "Reverend Dave." Names and some locations will be changed here to protect the innocent.

It was just a few years ago when Reverend Dave was appointed to the directorship of a church association that managed field trips, outdoor activities, and religious retreats for young people. The woman who hired him praised Dave for his vision, and his attention to detail. She noted his military service and volunteer work in the community. She described his job as one of "training our church's young people to be moral leaders in the modern world." She noted that Dave's superiors and coworkers in his present job gave him high marks across the board. "We are proud to have him on board," she told her congregants.

Reverend Dave's resume showed a man who seemed to be in love with the great outdoors. In his work he liked to share this enthusiasm with young people. He had coordinated camping trips, nature hikes, and retreats. These activities had brought him into contact with thousands of participants in several states. His record showed no sins, slip-ups, or difficulties. If you wanted a spiritual counselor for your outdoors-loving child, Dave seemed like the perfect choice.

Two years later, while conducting an investigation that seemed to have no relation to Reverend Dave, law enforcement officials found a set of eight images on the computer of a suspected child pornographer. Amidst a huge collection of graphic scenes of sex acts and violence, these pictures were different. The subjects were several boys ranging from ten to sixteen. Some were outdoor shots in what seemed to be vast, wide-open settings. Others were taken in hotel and motel bedrooms and bathrooms. None of the boys were engaged in sex, but some appeared to be uncomfortable as they struck provocative poses.

Investigators cross-referenced the photo set with images found online. According to one agent, they learned that this set of photos was being "distributed and traded by child pornography collectors on an international scale." They forwarded the images to the National Center for Missing and Exploited Children (NCMEC). This organization has built a huge database, cataloging prohibited images so they can be used in investigations. Once the images were cataloged, the investigators got on the internet to see what they could find. Though they wanted to find the pornographer, their first concern was what they had in front of them: the victims.

As we have already seen, many young victims of human trafficking enter that world by way of the commercial sex trade. The demand for this is huge, and ever-growing. The reasons are simple. First, the world is full of people who want sexual pleasure. Second, like alcohol, heroin, or any other habit-forming substance or behavior, artificial sexual pleasure becomes addicting.

Bestselling author and scholar Catherine MacKinnon has said: "[C]onsuming pornography is an experience of bought sex." She goes on to tell readers that pornography turns the victim into a seemingly inhuman object whose function is to gratify the viewer. Once hooked, the viewer has a growing hunger to buy or trade for sexual pleasure, and to act out any fantasies he might have when viewing the images. MacKinnon also observes that pornography serves to advertise whatever one might expect to get from victims. Traffickers see the victims as products, and the acts as services. If a user wants to go further, that can always be arranged.

The process of gratification through pornography changes the viewer's ideas about sex. Sexual gratification becomes something that is always available, and, as with narcotics, alcohol, and other addictions, a physical and psychological cycle develops. Viewers crave more sex, and they want their sexual experiences to be more titillating. To create a more intense experience a viewer will often seek out images of torture, bondage, and violence. Like drug addicts seeking greater highs, users need these escalations just to receive the same stimulation as they got from less disturbing images before their addiction built up.

Though the boys in the photos had been victimized, investigators had no way of knowing how far their exploiters had gone. The authorities had no idea who these boys were. The images were suggestive of sexual acts, including intimate bodily functions, and close-ups of genitalia, but none of them portrayed anyone engaged in sex.

Within the NCMEC is the Child Victim Identification Program (CVIP). As this agency's investigators joined the team, they brought in state-of-the-art digital tools to analyze and cross-reference the images. These agents had seen much worse, having dealt with many of the world's most disturbing visuals. But they all understood that, whatever the obvious content, soft porn images are often just the tip of a very ugly iceberg.

Though the images lacked any GPS tags, they did contain other evidence. They were dated, and the interior shots were mostly set in motel rooms. If agents could identify any of the motels, they could then check the registers on those dates, looking for rooms rented by men accompanied by boys.

Among the photos was a sub-group all taken in the same motel room a couple of summers earlier. Analysts compared these to visual data from motels all over the western United States. Using several clues and markers, they found a match in one of a chain of motels, this one in Amarillo, Texas. But when they looked at the register for the dates in question, none of the occupants raised any flags. For a long time, it looked as if the query had reached a dead end.

A year later something surfaced. In an unrelated investigation, analysts had turned up pictures of some of the same boys. Most of these were outdoor photos, taken in what were clearly western settings. These were dated just two days earlier than the photos they'd found before. Also, one photo revealed an identifiable landmark. The image was of the exterior of a motel in southwest Wyoming just off Route 80.

When they contacted the motel owner, he furnished them with registers and records of credit card transactions. Investigators pored through the information, found a few likely names, then searched these peoples' public social media pages. It didn't take long to find photos—albeit much more innocent shots—of some of the same boys, in the same places, matching the dates they were looking for. They then got a judge to issue a warrant to go further, in a more complete examination of Facebook data. Once they compared what they found with the motel records, they had their prime suspect. Reverend Dave had posted photos of a camping trip he'd taken with the boys in question. From there it was easy to identify some of the boys. Their Facebook pages had similar photos and other data.

Investigators found this forty-seven-year-old minister working for a group of affiliated churches that spread up and down the Pacific Coast. Reverend Dave directed their programs for youth retreats, summer camps, and other outdoor activities. Though his Facebook page looked innocent enough, it did correspond with the other evidence in one regard: Aside from Dave, the only people in the images were young boys.

There were numerous photos from the dates in question, but the search of Dave's postings revealed more. There were nude pictures of the boys from a trip the following spring, and from a hike that took place two years before the Wyoming photos. Dave also had social media pages under aliases. These turned up links to "the best places for nude camping," and others to child porn videos.

Many of the nude photos were collected in sets. Investigators found most of these sets circulating online among collectors of child pornography. Adults were mostly cropped out, while genitalia were often emphasized. In two photos the adult hadn't been completely excluded. In both the man was nude, but each was from the back. Nevertheless, a buttock scar matched a scar recorded on Dave's military records.

Investigators thought they were a week or two away from arresting Dave, but a discovery hurried their schedule. From his Facebook page they learned he was taking a trip that weekend with a lonely, troubled ninth grader. The two were flying to Asia with no specific date for their return. The next morning the investigators asked a judge to issue another warrant. That afternoon they raided Reverend Dave's home.

When they questioned Dave, he didn't deny collecting the photos, but he defended himself by saying he had never had sex with any of the boys. He said he used the pictures for his own private pleasure, and never "acted out" any of his fantasies. Then his interrogators focused on his upcoming trip. On his tablet Dave had a series of recent photos of the boy he planned to take overseas. Though the boy was the only subject, these pictures were more explicit and provocative than any Dave had taken before. When his questioners presented him with these, Dave began to weep. Nonetheless, he still denied any wrongdoing. He contended that the pictures weren't pornography because they didn't depict sex acts. Dave was wrong. Federal child pornography law prohibits "lascivious exhibition of the genitals or pubic area." This restriction can be used against pornographers who haven't touched their victims, or those whose "acting out" can't be proved beyond a reasonable doubt.

Some might wonder if these boys were truly abused. With no evidence of touching or physical contact, charges like "assault" or "rape" would be easy to counter. Though Dave had obviously exploited these boys, profiting from their images, he claimed he had never laid a finger on them. It's a claim his prosecutors can ignore. Their case doesn't rely on assault or rape. The images of these boys have been sold, bartered, and passed around the globe. That means these boys have become the objects of pedophile fantasies, with whatever that might imply. Dave, and others, have profited from this exploitation.

Reverend Dave is just one example of how pornography becomes a form of human trafficking. As cases go, his is less violent and less directly physically abusive than most. Some porn producers put together "stables" of performers—a captive group, each vying for better treatment. Some violent acts are faked, but others are quite real. In extreme cases, this can lead to the infamous snuff films where real torture leads to real murder.

Those who are sucked into a life of prostitution are often also exploited as pornographic slaves. Many pimps routinely film their victims' sexual encounters. Some victims are trafficked solely as porn performers. Others are like the boys Dave victimized, and have no idea that their images are being sold. In an era of webcams and social media, pornographers can easily blur the lines.

Some of us might be tempted to think that porn performers are simply workers in a somewhat shady, yet more and more accepted area of entertainment. This is one of the oldest arguments in the world for acquiescence. Providers argue: "People want it, so why shouldn't they get it?" But in these cases, "it" is sex between people who are often tricked, drugged, or otherwise coerced into acts of violence and abuse. This coercion fits every definition of human trafficking.

Some porn viewers turn to a more physical solution: seeking out prostitutes to fulfill their fantasies. As one anonymous commentator put it: "If prostitution is the main act, porn is the dress rehearsal." Some awareness of this is on display in the Trafficking Victims Protection Act of 2000 (TVPA). This law recognizes that those who are exploited in pornography are also victims of human trafficking.

Patterns of prostitution and pornography are often established early. Some captors control their child victims so well that these victims seem to live seemingly normal lives among the rest of us. Few would ever imagine that a child might be exploited for sex and pornography every day, and still show up for school on time.

One anonymous victim told her story to reporter Kaitlin Menza on www.marieclaire.com. "As far back as I can remember, I see cameras, adults touching me, giving me something to drink," says the victim. "My earliest memories are of being forced to pose for child pornography, of being sexually abused."

She describes growing up on the approach road to a busy interstate highway. Her captor sold her services at truck stops. Connecting through CB radio, these assailants were brutalizing this girl when she was six years old. She, and other young girls, were herded together in warehouses, injected with drugs, then pornographers dressed them in lingerie, and made them act out scripts.

"I don't remember protesting," she says. "I didn't know any better. It wasn't until maybe sixth grade, when I was socializing with other kids at their homes and with their families, that I realized my life wasn't like theirs. None of my friends went to warehouses. None of them were touched."

Her abuser had always framed the activities as a privilege that she should think of as fun. He told her she was special, and this was why she could have this honor. Since he seemed to want his actions to please her, she assumed he would allow her to stop any time she wanted. For once she'd guessed right. As soon as she protested, her abuser walked away and she never saw him again. She was twelve years old.

This young girl coped by immersing herself in her studies. Raised in a rural community where not many kids went to college, she set higher education as her goal. She managed to make friends, and even had a couple of boyfriends in high school. Eventually she did her graduate work in gender and cultural studies. Her research taught her that "[t]ruck stops are havens for child abuse." She discovered a group called: Truckers

Against Trafficking, dedicated to stopping these crimes. As she compared her findings to her own personal history, one of her more perceptive professors told her: "We study our pain."

This young woman learned that tragedies like hers grow from the same roots that nurture so many other criminal enterprises: power and money. Abusers seek a powerful feeling, and their payments make facilitators (pimps, photographers, and captors) rich. There's always someone in the group who has powerful connections. Regularly scheduled pedophile pornography parties aren't tolerated unless someone in power chooses to look the other way.

Now this former victim has her own preteen son, and she finds herself being extra vigilant. She's careful to separate suspicion from judgment, but she errs on the side of caution. "People's sixth senses about these things are often correct," she tells her interviewer. When she's discussing her abuser with people she knew growing up, she says they nod, and say something like: "Yeah, I always thought something was going on..." The first thought that screams through her mind is: "Why didn't you say anything?" That's her main message to all of us: You have to say something. You must ask questions.

Protecting our kids from predators is everyone's job. It is the only way we can keep kids from becoming someone else's slaves right under our noses.

WHEN SLAVES ARE FORCED TO FIGHT

"What they did to us should never be done to any human being."

-Grace Akallo, former child soldier

In some parts of the world the wars never stop. As one conflict ends, another starts. These wars destroy families, villages, tribes, and whole nations, yet even when the destruction seems complete, armies keep fighting. When the dust clears only poverty and chaos remain. Victims are left to roam through a devastated world where they no longer have a home.

This creates an insatiable appetite for soldiers. As armies run out of young fit men and women, they begin to take those who are less fit. When there's a shortage of these, commanders recruit children. This happens worldwide, but here we will concentrate on two examples from Uganda, where Joseph Kony's so-called "Lord's Resistance Army" made a specialty of recruiting young, impressionable boys and girls.

It was New Year's Day of 1994 when soldiers on a low-flying Ugandan Army helicopter sprayed gunfire into the tall grasses at the edge of a northern village. One of the village boys, Norman Okello, was twelve that day. Like most boys that age, he was full of energy, innocence, and ignorance. That made him a perfect candidate for Kony's army. Kony liked child recruits because they were easy to control. If he could use fear to channel their energy into violence, they could serve him well.

Kony's troops took Norman as the boy and his father were trying to escape the gunfire. They were sneaking home from the family's rice field just outside their village. Five men wearing stolen army uniforms surrounded them. Norman and his father knew the men's real loyalties from their telltale dreadlocks. These were Kony's rebels, famous for their murder and mayhem.

One of the soldiers asked Norman if the man with him was his father. "No, sir," Norman replied softly.

The soldier lifted a club and roared: "Tell me if this man is your father! Now!"

"He isn't," Norman lied, speaking up. He just hoped the men would believe him. He knew he must lie if his father was to have any chance at survival. If their captors thought this man was his father, they would kill him, or try to force Norman to kill him. This was a standard policy in Kony's army. If children had no parents to return to, they were less prone to try to escape. If a child killed his or her own parent, it was like destroying the child's mental home. It was Kony's aim to own these children. Killing their loved ones shocked them into subservience.

Somehow Norman convinced the soldiers of his lie. Two men led his father down the road to a spot where Norman could still see him in the distance. The others presented Norman to their local commander, a man named Ojara. Ojara was accompanied by four mean-looking teenagers. On orders from their commander, they approached the boy with sticks. Just before they started beating Norman, Ojara said: "If you scream, they will kill you."

As his father watched helplessly from far away, Ojara's teenagers beat Norman senseless. "My face swelled up; my eyes bled. By the end, you could not recognize me," he told an interviewer many years later.

Norman was still wearing his school shorts when the soldiers dragged him away. He was theirs now. Later he recalled: "I totally lost any hope in anything."

This was the first step in his indoctrination: cut a boy off from his family and beat the spirit out of him.

All military training has an element of stripping a person bare. In a reasonably decent, honest culture this is usually done with some underlying respect for the individual. Basic military training is meant to teach a recruit how to fit into a unit and obey every order. He or she must learn this discipline because the lives of everyone in the unit might depend on this person someday. The superior's unstated respect for the recruit stems from an understanding that without some sense of self, a soldier can't take initiative. Good military training recognizes that there will be times when a soldier is cut off from superiors. At such a moment a good soldier must be ready to make the right decision.

Joseph Kony has little understanding of this balance between discipline and independence. That's one reason his "revolution" has all but failed. As of this writing his once-dangerous army of thousands is down to less than a hundred, but for two decades his marauding bands spread death and destruction all over northern Uganda. When he gained control of large areas, Kony ruled through fear. He stirred up nightmares in his child soldiers, then encouraged them to turn these nightmares into reality. When these children thought village leaders might report their location to government authorities, they would spear and padlock the chiefs' lips together. To control people's movements Kony banned bicycles, so when the child soldiers caught someone riding a bike, they cut off the rider's legs and buttocks.

After the soldiers had beaten Norman to a pulp, they revived him. Pain was like an ever-growing weight throughout his body. Once he could walk, they prodded him along on a three-day march. There were many other boys marching with them; some were worse off than Norman. He later told an interviewer: "They'd say, 'Do you want a rest?' If you say 'yes', they take you under a tree and kill you.'"

Soldiers told the boys they were "unclean," and made them eat alone. On the fourth day they decided Norman could join them at mealtimes, but first they had to initiate him. With a mixture of shea oil and water they put the sign of the cross on his head, lips, hands, and heart. He was no longer unclean. These older boys (most were still in their teens) accepted him. After all he'd been through, it felt good.

Two months later his captors forced him to kill someone. The eighteen-year-old victim they selected was a an LRA veteran who had tried to escape. Norman didn't have to do the job alone. This execution would be a group effort. At that point he had become one in a group of three hundred new recruits. All these boys were near starvation, tired, and thirsty. Their captors were marching them through the hills to an LRA base just across the northern border.

Their commander brought out the "traitor," and directed the boys to an array of weapons, telling them to pick whichever one they wanted. "Some picked clubs, some picked machetes, some picked an ax," Norman told his interviewer. "Me, I picked a bayonet." Then each boy was given his chance at the condemned man. Some stabbed, some hacked, some bludgeoned. Norman had selected a bayonet. By the time his turn came, the victim was barely moving. Norman pierced the soldier's chest and heard his last breath. "Out of being innocent, you've now become guilty," he told his interviewer. "You feel like you're becoming part of them, part of the rebels."

In his first days as a soldier Norman still looked for a chance to escape, but eventually his imagination failed him. He had no notion of where his home had been, or if it still existed. "You say, 'I will die like this,'" he told his interviewer. "You give up." This was a surrender to hunger, forced marches, and violent atrocities. Norman watched as one man was sliced up alive, ending up in small pieces. He soon realized that he could only survive by not thinking about his home and family. Thinking of them made him feel ill. He realized that any real illness would probably kill him. In the end his will to survive won out.

Like all Kony's child soldiers, Norman was beaten regularly. His captors did this to keep his anger sharp, and to make him want to hurt others. In addition, Kony and his lieutenants brainwashed the boys, immersing them in what was really a kind of pseudo-religious cult. Each day Norman would see Kony preaching his strange doctrines to crowds numbering in the hundreds. The man stood, speaking all day, mixing politics, gods, and cultural icons into his rants. His face would twist, his voice growing louder, as his thoughts became more and violent. This inspired respect in some ignorant minds. It was thought that "a common man could not speak from morning until sunset while standing," Norman observed.

Norman saw far too many horrors to list here. He was often one of the soldiers who were perpetrating them. He was reduced to mindlessness about anything but his own survival. "What I always said was, you should enjoy killing your enemies," he recalled, "because if you don't enjoy killing them, then your enemies will enjoy killing you."

Much later Norman spilled out his story to a representative of a Christian aid organization named Theo Hollander. It was the first step in a years-long recovery. Even a decade later the nightmares were enough to make him fear falling asleep. The young man suffered bouts of panic and anger. Whenever he felt like destroying something, or hurting someone, his solution was to run the other way.

As time passed, Norman learned that his traumatic experience was depressingly ordinary in his part of the world. It's estimated that Kony's army recruited nearly forty thousand children in much the same way they'd recruited him. With a great deal of counseling and retraining many of the survivors have returned to peaceful, normal lives.

At this writing, Norman has recovered, and he is now the father of two children. "I'm normal now. I'm just another member of the community. But the nightmare is there. I dream about someone coming to abduct me."

Another of Kony's child soldiers was Grace Akallo. To this day she still expresses her hope that he will be captured and brought to justice before she dies. But she has thought beyond that, and she asks: "What is the next step?" Grace was captured when she was fifteen — taken from a Catholic school where she was boarding. The girls had been trained to run outside and hide if Kony's troops ever invaded the school. They had drilled, and each girl had a designated place to take cover. "It was very scary," she said later. "[A nun] would come in and say, 'Girls, we have to run right now.'" One night, when it wasn't a drill, the soldiers caught her.

After her abduction Grace had training much like Norman's. She went on forced marches, starved, was beaten, and was forced to beat others. When a male soldier wanted sex, a girl submitted. They called it "becoming a wife." Kony convinced the girls he could read their minds and knew when they had thoughts of escaping.

Eventually Grace passed out during a pitched battle. When the battle was over, her fellow soldiers thought she was dead, and put her in a hole with some corpses, tossing a little dirt on top. After they left, she emerged, and started her long journey home. Yet she had to fear everyone she encountered. "Sometimes the community would decide to beat you or kill you or report you that you were a rebel. We feared the community and the Ugandan soldiers."

For a time, she felt estranged from her family, but eventually she started telling her experiences to a nun. This helped, but Grace knows that not everything can be solved by talking. These children are starting life over again. They must acclimate themselves to school, family, and work as if all these things were new and unfamiliar experiences. In many ways everything is new to someone getting his or her first taste of freedom.

As of this writing Kony's army has been reduced to a ragged band of outlaws, but there are many others like him all over the world. These warlords engage in the kind of wholesale slavery requiring a level of organization and force usually possessed only by real nations. They raise armies, control territory, and spread fear. They enslave young bodies and minds in ways that leave permanent marks, both physical and psychological. Everyone must oppose them. We must join together to let our leaders know that we demand the removal of these warlords from the community of nations. Only then will this kind of enslavement stop.

GROWING UP WITH A SLAVE

"The blunting effects of slavery upon the slaveholder's moral perceptions are known and conceded the world over."

-Mark Twain

Different people imagine slavery in different ways. For a century after the Civil War many white folks here in the U.S. imagined slavery as it was portrayed in stories like *Gone with the Wind*. In this false fantasy the enslaved African-Americans were seen as lesser beings, content to serve their white masters. Whites assumed that enslaved African-Americans had usually been treated with kindness, but even in that whitewashed picture white folks always had control. For the last half-century whites have been slowly giving up this picture, but inherent racism keeps it alive, even though many whites know better.

African-Americans have inherited a more realistic viewpoint. They understand the brutality and sheer inhumanity of the peculiarly evil institution. It was their not-so-distant ancestors who had to endure beatings, lashings, and the oppression of an entire social system constructed for the benefit of the whites who held them captive.

With a history like ours, we might hope that real slavery would be nothing but a memory in our country. As we have seen in earlier chapters, this is not true. We have recounted the horrors of human trafficking, and how it enslaves its victims for pornography, prostitution, soldiering, housekeeping, and work in farms and factories. These are intentional crimes committed for profit. But many situations that involve enslavement are less overt. The person who enslaves others may be consciously committing a wrong, but anyone with awareness of this crime becomes an accomplice simply by accepting what's already there. Even with an issue as horrific as human slavery, there can be gray areas.

In an article in *The Atlantic Monthly* the late Alex Tizon, grandson of an American officer/planter in the Philippines, recounted his experience growing up in the shadow of enslavement. A part of his coming-of-age was facing the saddest part of his upbringing: that of his family's effective ownership of another human being. This ownership wasn't legal, but Tizon's parents understood. They owned a human being who believed her entire existence hinged on her ability to serve them.

"Her name was Eudocia Tomas Pulido," Tizon wrote. "We called her Lola. She was four foot eleven, with mocha-brown skin and almond eyes that I can still see looking into mine—my first memory."

Tizon's grandfather, Tomas Asuncion, was an American army officer in the Philippines. "Lieutenant Tom," as he was called, bought a lot of land, settled down, and ran his plantation. Tizon describes Lieutenant Tom as "formidable" and "given to dark moods." Tom's Filipino wife died giving birth to Tizon's mother. As a result, the little girl was brought up by native "utusans" which translates: "people who take commands."

When World War II came, Tom knew he would have to join his fellow Americans fighting the

Japanese. This meant he had to leave his twelve-year-old daughter at home. After some scouting, he found Lola, a young woman from a very poor family distantly related to his wife. Lola's family had promised her in marriage to an elderly man who could barely support her, but these arrangements hadn't been finalized. Tom offered Lola an alternative: the job of taking care of his daughter. He never told her that the position was permanent, but tradition, and subsequent events, proved this to be true. Tom described her to his daughter as "a gift." The young girl didn't want this gift, but once she had Lola, she came to depend on her for everything, tacitly confirming the nature of their relationship. Once Tom arrived home for an unexpected visit and discovered his daughter had been talking to a boy he didn't like. When he announced that her penalty would be a whipping, she knew that tradition gave her an out. She asked that she be allowed to stand by while her "gift" took the punishment for. Lola withstood twelve hard lashes without a word. With each lash, Lieutenant Tom repeated to his daughter that she must never lie to him. Decades later, when the grown-up girl told her son this story, she seemed to relish its outrageousness.

In 1950, Tizon's parents married, giving him a half-caste mother and a Filipino father. The following year the couple had a son whom they named Arthur. That same year "haunted by demons," Lieutenant Tom committed suicide. Tizon was his parents' second child, arriving in 1959. Three more siblings followed. In 1964, his father was offered a job in the States. Tizon's parents wanted Lola to come with them, but for once she expressed misgivings. It was so far away, and she worried that they would never let her return to their home. Tizon's father painted a rosy picture. Though his stateside salary would be modest, he promised there would be money. Lola would receive an allowance, much of which she could send home. That way she could help her parents build a concrete house to replace their fragile hut. These promises convinced her, and the family brought her along.

Life in the States was better for the Tizons, but not as easy as they thought. Tizon's mother, a qualified doctor, took a job as a technician in a medical lab, while his father worked two jobs to make ends meet. Two years after they arrived, Lola asked about her allowance. She'd gotten word that her mother was sick and needed medicine. "How could you even ask?" his father responded in Tagalog. "You see how hard up we are. Don't you have any shame?"

Tizon was only four when his family came here— too young to understand the nuances of enslavement. But he witnessed its harsh effects on Lola, and the way it brought out the worst side in his parents. If the housework wasn't done to their specifications, they berated her until she was reduced to tears.

Tizon's brother, Arthur, first introduced the idea of "slave" to his younger sibling. They'd grown up with a growing awareness that something was deeply wrong in the family's relationship with Lola. They knew that her status was the source of the problem, and they began to understand how vulnerable and powerless she was. They also realized that she remained in her position due to ignorance, pain, and the implied threats of their parents. Tizon summarized Arthur's description of Lola's condition this way: "Wasn't paid. Toiled every day. Was tongue-lashed for sitting too long or falling asleep too early. Was struck for talking back. Wore hand-me-downs. Ate scraps and leftovers by herself in the kitchen. Rarely left the house. Had no friends or hobbies outside the family. Had no private quarters." Gradually both boys were coming to the conclusion that the whole situation was immoral. "It confused me . . . " Tizon wrote. "Having a slave gave me grave doubts about what kind of people we were, what kind of place we came from."

Once, when Tizon was sick and too weak to eat, Lola chewed his food for him before putting it in his mouth. Those of us from the developed world might find this gross or unsanitary, but the boy digested it, and gained strength. When any of the children were ill, she took care of them. When the family was hungry, she fed them. When the house was dirty, she cleaned it. Laundry, sewing, and garbage disposal were her responsibilities. If she failed, she drew harsh words; if she succeeded no one noticed.

Tizon remembered how badly his parents treated Lola in the Philippines, then added: "In America, they treated her worse but took pains to conceal it." When she served their guests his parents always audibly thanked her. When she served only the family this gratitude disappeared. Once Tizon's best friend walked in on a bad situation. Tizon's mother was shouting at Lola, who cowered in a corner. It was one of many moments that Tizon had to explain away. Despite these explanations Tizon's friend remained suspicious, but he didn't guess the secret.

To friends and neighbors Lola was an aunt, cousin, or some more distant relation. She was "shy," or "quiet," or "backward." But to Tizon's mother, Lola had become a necessity and a crime. Neither parent had enough time for their children. Eventually Tizon's father walked out. In the 1970s, Lola got word that her mother had died, then her father. She wanted to go home and see her family, but the time was never right. Money was short, the kids needed her, etc. etc.

The real reason for their refusal to let her leave was Lola's immigration status. Her work papers had expired in 1969. If the authorities had found out, and deported her, the whole family might have met the same fate.

After Tizon's father deserted the family, his mother sometimes teetered on the edge of breakdown. Tizon witnessed moments when his mother's "gift" soothed and comforted her mistress. When Tizon's mother got remarried to an abusive husband, it was Lola who protected her, staring down this 250-pound man, and silencing him by simply uttering his name.

The Tizons' ownership of Lola eroded their sense of family. As the children began to take Lola's side, their mother accused her of intentionally stealing their loyalty. When Lola's teeth started falling out, their mother blamed her for her own malady. "That's what happens when you don't brush properly," she told Lola. When Tizon confronted his mother, and accused her of treating Lola as a slave, his mother contended that none of her children could possibly understand her relationship with Lola.

The author's sister, Tizon Quillen, reacted to her brother's article with sorrow and resignation. "It was a strange relationship between my mother and Lola," she says. "She was devoted to my mother until she died. Lola would tell us, 'Stop trying to make me leave your mother!' when we wanted to get her a better life or offered to take her back to the Philippines. We were frustrated because we hated seeing her abused, but in her psyche, she couldn't leave, because she was so dedicated."

When Tizon's mother died, Lola was at her side. Afterward she moved in with Tizon, who now had children of his own. In her last years she took up gardening, and even taught herself to read. At Tizon's urging, she visited her home in the Philippines, but found that much had changed. She thought she might want to go back there to die, but that would be in the future, if it happened at all. In the end she returned to the States, where she died five years later. Soon after her death Tizon carried her ashes back to her home village.

Lola's story shows that one of the saddest things about slavery is the way it forces us to lie to ourselves. Though we might understand that it's a problem somewhere, we avoid the notion that it could ever touch us or our families. One of the biggest obstacles to dealing with slavery is that it hides in plain sight. It's there among women and girls soliciting sex on a street corner. We tell ourselves that these exploited women have gotten where they are by making poor choices, but many had no choice at all. We find slavery on display at border crossings, in porn films, or on the battlefield, but we train ourselves to see illegal immigrants, highly sexed movies, or bloodthirsty soldiers. Many of the people we regard as villains are enslaved pawns who have little choice in what they do.

Some slave stories are like Lola's. She fell from one sad situation into another. She was trained into slavery, learning to subvert her desires so she could serve others. Yet in the end her heart and soul remained free. That was why she could calm a sad child or soothe a troubled wife and mother. It was the reason she could stop a man more than twice her size by simply uttering his name. In her last years, when she was finally given her liberty, she showed her true self to the Tizons. She cooked, gardened, and traveled across the world's widest ocean to see her home again. When she returned to her family's village, she had no urge to stay.

Lola was seventy-five before she was given the chance to become her own woman, but even at that advanced age she knew who she'd always wanted to be. That's what human slavery takes from a person: the ability to be one's true self. It's the duty of every free citizen to give it back.

Slavery can slowly infect a family. Most of us think we know the difference between an employee who freely takes a job, and a person who's enslaved, but Tizon's experience shows how easily that difference can fade into gray areas. It might start with parents hiring a live-in servant. The servant gets room and board, which helps them justify a pay rate below minimum. The parents skip a paycheck, promising to provide any cash the servant really needs. Years pass, and gradually the "servant" becomes an essential part of the family's home. With little or no spending money, the servant becomes a captive to the situation. Somewhere he or she has crossed an invisible line into involuntary servitude—a legal phrase for slavery.

Sometimes the process is more formal and businesslike, but the degradation is still there. In an article at vice.com Hina Husain recalls the servants her family had in Pakistan: "There was an unspoken understanding between the servants and their employers—my family—the servants were there only to provide for the family and their needs, nothing else. You didn't make friends with your servants. You didn't talk to them freely or treat them in a way that was too welcoming or warm. You always had to maintain an emotional and mental distance from them because they were not your equals. They existed only to facilitate your life, nothing more."

One American who originally came from the Philippines, M. Evelina Galang, carefully measured her response to reading Tizon's story. Galang had grown up in an upper-class household where servants were a normal part of life. She recognizes the problem but believes there are complexities that Tizon hasn't addressed. She sees his story as the opening of a dialogue. Concluding her own contribution, she writes: "I do not condone the circumstances of how the Tizon family treated [Lola]. But Alex Tizon inherited this story. He had a long struggle to make sense of it before he died at the age of fifty-seven. He might have written it in his diaries and kept it to himself, but he did not. He put it out there, and his story, even to the end, is messy. The conversation around Tizon's essay is important. It will take time, and it may be a struggle to shift cultural attitudes about servitude in the Philippines, but the awareness around [Lola] is a start."

These stories and comments highlight the fact that all efforts to end slavery and human trafficking begin with us. For some of us the work will begin within our own homes and families. Slavery in the home often starts in seeming innocence. Our guilt comes when we close our eyes, enlist willful ignorance as our partner, and allow the behavior of enslavement to slowly infect our lives.

SOLUTIONS FOR THE VARIETIES OF HUMAN TRAFFICKING

"I alone cannot change the world, but I can cast a stone across the waters to create many ripples."

-Mother Teresa

Human trafficking takes many forms and serves all kinds of functions. Children are recruited to beg in the streets. Talented young people are enslaved for sport, becoming boxers, camel jockeys, footballers, or even prey for hunters. Domestic servants, prostitutes, and farmhands can all find victims of human trafficking within their ranks.

At this writing, in late July of 2017, human trafficking is in the news. This past weekend a tractor-trailer pulled into a San Antonio parking lot. After it had parked, some passersby heard sounds from inside. When the back was opened, people spilled out, some running, some crawling. Inside were the dead and near dead. According to San Antonio Fire Chief Charles Hood: "[The victims] were very hot to the touch..." Apparently, no one had provided these people with water in quite a while.

Details of this case are still emerging. Survivors say there may have been as many as one hundred people stuffed into the trailer. When the dust cleared, thirty-seven were still there and breathing. Eight were dead, and two more died at the hospital. Though the immigrants had been told the trailer had refrigeration, they soon learned that the cooling unit was broken. Though the walls should have had vent holes, all but one was blocked. Though the ride should've been short, it lasted for hours.

So far, the driver has professed ignorance of his cargo, but the immigrants inside are representative of the tragedy of human trafficking. Smugglers bring them in, then the traffickers transport them to various destinations. One group in the trailer had paid members of a drug cartel to protect them as they crossed the Rio Grande on a raft. Another band of hopeful immigrants had been crammed into a Laredo "stash house" for days before the truck arrived. A survivor had been told he was headed for Minnesota.

At least four of them were between the ages of ten and seventeen. None of these people really knew where they were going. They crammed themselves into hot darkness, hoping that this was just a hellish moment on the road to the American Dream. Instead they were descending into a nightmare.

Though the San Antonio case is big, it's not unusual. In the past month at least four truck seizures have been reported in and around Laredo, Texas. Seventy-two people were trapped in one truck. All had recently arrived from Mexico, Ecuador, Guatemala, and El Salvador.

With the hundreds of miles of border between Texas and Mexico, the business of human smuggling seems almost unstoppable; so does the trafficking of the captive cargos once they arrive here. Tragic ends like the one in the San Antonio parking lot are on the upswing. Some critics blame harsh new immigration policies. Bob Libal, executive director of the Austin-based nonprofit, Grassroots Leadership, told reporters:

"These tragedies are compounded when [immigration is] incredibly dangerous and incredibly expensive . . . Everyone's thoughts today should be not in politicizing it, but in making sure that everyone who survived this ordeal is treated with respect and gets the protection they need."

The current acting director for Immigration and Customs Enforcement, Thomas Homan, doesn't contest the fact that these victims deserve respect, but he also believes that the most humane solution is to deter potential crossers from paying criminals to help them get here. "Why am I so strong in what I'm trying to do?" Homan asks. "Because people haven't seen what Tom Homan's seen. They haven't seen the dead immigrants on a trail that were left stranded . . . People weren't standing with me in Victoria, Texas, in the back of a tractor-trailer with nineteen dead aliens including a five-year-old child lying dead under his father that suffocated." Homan worked that case fourteen years ago. It convinced him that one solution to human trafficking is to stop the illegal importation of human cargo, and send its victims back to their homes, where they can try a legal route. The only trouble is that they already know legal entry is next to impossible.

What can we do to stop them? Any effective effort must begin with individuals. Most of us have seen some aspect of this crime. It might be the nanny in a friend's home, or kitchen staffers at a local restaurant. Some might encounter it in a downloaded porn video or see a truckload of undocumented day laborers arriving at a construction site. This is not to say that you should call in the authorities every time you see a situation where you suspect trafficking might play a role. You don't have to turn in the nanny or your friend. But you might talk to them. You can also watch those kitchen staffers or construction workers to see if they show any signs of abuse, coercion, or other crimes to which they might fall victim. As for the porn video—simply don't go there. Besides the more obvious reasons, you should consider that with every click you're increasing their ad revenue. Those profits keep pornographers and their fellow human traffickers in business.

We can all advocate for better laws. Some proposals target the traffickers themselves. Laws and policies that reward victims for exposing their traffickers can be effective and humane at the same time.

Another thing you can do is to support organizations that oppose human trafficking. Here are a few:

The Polaris Project provides services and support for trafficking victims and works with survivors to develop long-term strategies to ending human trafficking.

Children's Organization of Southeast Asia (COSA) provides education, intervention, and support in the hard-hit Hill tribe communities in Thailand. Many of their education initiatives target the traffickers themselves, many of whom are ignorant of trafficking's consequences.

California Against Slavery advocates for victims of human trafficking in California, and throughout the world.

Ricky Martin Foundation which supports children's causes all over the globe.

Vital Voices—an international nonprofit NGO working with women leaders to further economic empowerment, women's political participation, and human rights.

Governments must commit themselves to enforcing laws against trafficking within their nations' borders. Human traffickers must be caught and prosecuted. Their victims need medical and psychological support, along with financial aid and education. We should support efforts in the UN and other international organizations, promoting their work in healing victims and stopping their traffickers.

All of us must get involved. We must root out support for human trafficking in our own communities. This means educating business owners, parents, and kids, identifying sources and consumers of child pornography, and enforcing legal hiring practices among local companies.

Human Trafficking is a huge obstacle to human progress. Still, we can end it one family and community at a time. Each of us must pledge ourselves to standing up for victims. We should spread warnings in our schools, find guidance in our churches, and identify our allies in law enforcement.

If we foster the idea that people must always come before profits, and if we consistently stand up for what's right, we can halt the eroding effects of human trafficking in our communities. From there we can change people's thinking and behavior throughout the country, and even the world.

ABOUT THE AUTHOR

Malcolm Allen is a recognized expert on human potential and (BCSA) Board Certified Social Advocate. He migrates effortlessly between corporate boardrooms and underserved communities aiming to advance the interests of social justice, particularly on behalf of populations or groups who have been disadvantaged, disempowered, or forgotten.

Allen has authored over two dozen books, and most have achieved best-selling status. He has worked with subject matter experts and credentialed instruction designers to socially engineer a platform of outcome-based programs that provide solutions for disabled veterans, recidivism, human trafficking, dropout prevention, bullying, diversity, mentoring, financial inclusion, entrepreneurship, and leadership. All programs are Military Approved, and available at Penn Foster College and Graduate America Centers of Excellence around the world. For seminar licensing, book purchases, or speaker requests, please visit: Unconditional.org